Creation

An Introduction

Tyler R. Wittman

CROSSWAY®
WHEATON, ILLINOIS

Creation: An Introduction

Published by Crossway
1300 Crescent Street
Wheaton, Illinois 60187

Cover design: Jordan Singer

First printing 2025

Printed in the United States of America

Trade paperback ISBN: 978-1-4335-7926-4
ePub ISBN: 978-1-4335-7929-5
PDF ISBN: 978-1-4335-7927-1

Library of Congress Cataloging-in-Publication Data

Names: Wittman, Tyler, author.
Title: Creation : an introduction / Tyler R. Wittman.
Description: Wheaton, Illinois : Crossway, [2025] | Series: Short studies in systematic theology | Includes bibliographical references and index.
Identifiers: LCCN 2025009430 (print) | LCCN 2025009431 (ebook) | ISBN 9781433579264 (trade paperback) | ISBN 9781433579271 (pdf) | ISBN 9781433579295 (epub)
Subjects: LCSH: Creation. | Trinity.
Classification: LCC BL227 .W58 2025 (print) | LCC BL227 (ebook) | DDC 231.7/65—dc23/eng/20250417
LC record available at https://lccn.loc.gov/2025009430
LC ebook record available at https://lccn.loc.gov/2025009431

Crossway is a publishing ministry of Good News Publishers.

VP 34 33 32 31 30 29 28 27 26 25
15 14 13 12 11 10 9 8 7 6 5 4 3 2 1

Creation

SHORT STUDIES IN SYSTEMATIC THEOLOGY

Edited by Graham A. Cole and Oren R. Martin

The Atonement: An Introduction, Jeremy Treat (2023)

The Attributes of God: An Introduction, Gerald Bray (2021)

The Church: An Introduction, Gregg R. Allison (2021)

Creation: An Introduction, Tyler R. Wittman (2025)

The Doctrine of Scripture: An Introduction, Mark D. Thompson (2022)

Glorification: An Introduction, Graham A. Cole (2022)

The Holy Spirit: An Introduction, Fred Sanders (2023)

Justification: An Introduction, Thomas R. Schreiner (2023)

The Person of Christ: An Introduction, Stephen J. Wellum (2021)

Predestination: An Introduction, Andrew David Naselli (2024)

Theological Method: An Introduction, Graham A. Cole (2025); formerly titled *Faithful Theology: An Introduction* (2020)

The Trinity: An Introduction, Scott R. Swain (2020)

"Drawing from the Tolkienian image of creation as song, this book offers an extremely useful and much-needed overview of the doctrine of creation. Whereas much contemporary reflection on creation draws its energy from real or perceived clashes with modern science, Wittman takes us back to the riches of historical theology and Scripture. From this angle, he enlarges our vision to see all that is involved in creation: the Trinity, creatureliness, sin, and the eschaton. Put simply, this book puts the focus where it belongs and does so with a fresh and amazingly well-informed deployment of the Christian tradition. Highly recommended for all Christians. I will certainly be reading whatever Wittman writes next!"

Gavin Ortlund, President, Truth Unites; Theologian in Residence, Immanuel Nashville, Tennessee; Visiting Professor of Historical Theology, Phoenix Seminary

"Creation reflects the musicality of God, and in this wonderful little book, Tyler Wittman equips readers to recognize, delight in, and even join in God's great song of creation. This song centers on the incarnate Christ and affirms the fullness of God's creative and redemptive energies. If you have not yet started thinking about the importance of the doctrine of creation, now is the time, and this is a great place to begin!"

Kelly M. Kapic, Professor of Theological Studies, Covenant College

"A substantive introduction to the doctrine of creation. Wittman's creative use of song sings as he harmonizes the various aspects of creation into a thoroughly biblical and historically grounded analysis. Wittman reminds us that theology should be doxological as it casts our vision to God and his action. Allow this book to tune your heart to sing the new song of grace, giving glory to the God who created all things."

Kyle Strobel, Director of the Institute for Spiritual Formation, Talbot School of Theology, Biola University

"God's people are meant to praise God not just for *some* of his works but for *all* of them. We worship God not just because he has saved us but also because he has made us. In this work, Tyler Wittman explores the good news of God the Creator. This book will help the church because it is both theologically rich and pastorally accessible."

J. T. English, Lead Pastor, Storyline Church, Arvada, Colorado; Associate Professor of Christian Theology, The Southern Baptist Theological Seminary; author, *Deep Discipleship*

"Tyler Wittman guides us to understand creation aright. He introduces us afresh to what it means to be a creature. He also shows why our creatureliness is gracious good news as he reflects on the wonder of God as our Creator. To know self, world, and God better, take and read this little gem of a book."

Michael Allen, John Dyer Trimble Professor of Systematic Theology and Academic Dean, Reformed Theological Seminary, Orlando

"As depicted in Psalm 148, creation is a vast yet ordered antiphonal choir, the creatures of the heavens and the earth arrayed in their distinct groups, each with a unique voice, united and harmonizing in a single song of praise. Wittman offers us an exhilarating exploration of this pregnant image for our understanding of creation, Christ's redemption, and our calling. His stimulating articulation of the doctrine moves his readers seamlessly into doxology."

Alastair J. Roberts, coauthor, *Echoes of Exodus*; Cohost, *Mere Fidelity* podcast

Poetry is the mother-tongue of the human race,
as the garden is older than the ploughed field;
painting, than writing; song, than declamation.

J. G. HAMANN, *AESTHETICA IN NUCE*

Remember to extol his work,
of which men have sung.

JOB 36:24

Contents

Series Preface ix

Abbreviations xi

Introduction: Creation as Song 1

1 The Song's Doxological Nature 11
The Creation Hymn

2 God's Musicality 39
The Trinity and Creation

3 How God Sings 61
Creation Out of Nothing and the Creator's Generosity

4 The Song's Melody 79
Hearing and Receiving God's Creative Word

5 The Frustrated Orchestra 101
Humans and Other Creatures

6 The Song's Resolution 121
Creation's Fulfillment in Christ

7 "I Will Sing and Make Melody to the LORD" 145
Gratitude and Sacrifice

Coda: Psalm 148 165

Acknowledgments 167

Glossary........ 169
Further Reading........ 171
General Index........ 173
Scripture Index........ 179

Series Preface

The ancient Greek thinker Heraclitus reputedly said that the thinker has to listen to the essence of things. A series of theological studies dealing with the traditional topics that make up systematic theology needs to do just that. Accordingly, in each of these studies, a theologian addresses the essence of a doctrine. This series thus aims to present short studies in theology that are attuned to both the Christian tradition and contemporary theology in order to equip the church to faithfully understand, love, teach, and apply what God has revealed in Scripture about a variety of topics. What may be lost in comprehensiveness can be gained through what John Calvin, in the dedicatory epistle of his commentary on Romans, called "lucid brevity."

Of course, a thorough study of any doctrine will be longer rather than shorter, as there are two millennia of confession, discussion, and debate with which to interact. As a result, a short study needs to be more selective but deftly so. Thankfully, the contributors to this series have the ability to be brief yet accurate. The key aim is that the simpler is not to morph into the simplistic. The test is whether the topic of a short study, when further studied in depth, requires some unlearning to take place. The simple can be amplified. The simplistic needs to be corrected. As editors, we believe that the volumes in this series pass that test.

While the specific focus varies, each volume (1) introduces the doctrine, (2) sets it in context, (3) develops it from Scripture, (4) draws the various threads together, and (5) brings it to bear on the Christian life. It is our prayer, then, that this series will assist the church to delight in her triune God by thinking his thoughts—which he has graciously revealed in his written word, which testifies to his living Word, Jesus Christ—after him in the powerful working of his Spirit.

Graham A. Cole and Oren R. Martin

Abbreviations

CO	*Ioannis Calvini opera omnia quae supersunt*
FC	Fathers of the Church
LCL	Loeb Classical Library
LNTS	The Library of New Testament Studies
LW	*Luther's Works*, American edition, ed. Jaroslav Pelikan and Helmut T. Lehmann, 55 vols. (Muhlenberg; Fortress; Concordia, 1955–1986)
LXX	Septuagint
NSBT	New Studies in Biblical Theology
PPS	Popular Patristics Series
WSA	*The Works of Saint Augustine: A New Translation for the 21st Century*, ed. John E. Rotelle et al. (New City Press, 1990–)

Introduction

Creation as Song

What is creation? If asked, many Christians would start listing things that populate our world: birds and bees, lizards and longhorns, fields and forests. Large things like mountains and oceans certainly come to mind. We'd think of the earth and, beyond that, the dancing spheres and burning stars within the great expanse. Eventually we'd think of ourselves and perhaps even our invisible neighbors, the angels and spirits. All of these answers are true, of course, but they don't so much answer the question as restate it. Examples of creatures don't help us define creation itself. So, again, what makes all of these things *creation*? The short answer is that they're all part of the Creator's song.

J. R. R. Tolkien understood that creation is song. Consider his creation myth for the world in which he would place Middle-Earth, found in *The Silmarillion*. Tolkien depicts the Creator, Ilúvatar, forging the world's existence through the music of his angels, the Ainur. Ilúvatar teaches them how to sing and eventually teaches them a "great theme" so they can "make in harmony together a Great Music" kindled by "Imperishable

Flame." As the Ainur sing Ilúvatar's theme, writes Tolkien, "a sound arose of endless interchanging melodies woven into harmony that passed beyond hearing into the depths and into the heights, and the places of the dwelling of Ilúvatar were filled to overflowing, and the music went out into the Void, and it was not void." The result: "Great beauty has been wakened into song."[1]

However, the mightiest of the Ainur, Melkor, soon devises his own additions to this flawless song.

> As the theme progressed, it came into the heart of Melkor to interweave matters of his own imagining that were not in accord with the theme of Ilúvatar; for he sought therein to increase the power and glory of the part assigned to himself. . . . Some of these thoughts he now wove into his music, and straightway discord arose about him, and many that sang nigh him grew despondent, and their thought was disturbed and their music faltered; but some began to attune their music to his rather than to the thought which they had at first.

Melkor's discordant variation spreads until Ilúvatar introduces a "new theme . . . like and yet unlike to the former theme, and it gathered power and had new beauty."[2]

Eventually, Ilúvatar overtakes Melkor's music by weaving his own new themes into the chaos, resolving its sorrow and ugliness by subsuming them as counterpoints in a theme of unforeseen harmony, beauty, and strength. Melkor's music is ultimately undone because it is loud, vain, and repetitive and, writes Tolkien, "had little harmony, but rather a clamorous

1. J. R. R. Tolkien, "Ainulindalë: The Music of the Ainur," in *The Silmarillion: The Myths and Legends of Middle-Earth*, ed. Christopher Tolkien (Houghton Mifflin, 1998), 15.
2. Tolkien, "The Music of the Ainur," 16.

unison as of many trumpets braying upon a few notes."[3] It loses out because it lacks beauty.

The "Song" Metaphor in Christian Tradition

Tolkien's myth is evocative and draws upon his own Christian tradition. Anticipating Ilúvatar's "new theme," Clement of Alexandria speaks of Christ as the "new song" bearing God's name, a "Levitical song," which is to say, the fulfilment of the music of the Levites, whom David appointed to sing during worship (cf. 1 Chron. 6:31–48) and who bore God's name on their foreheads (Ex. 28:36–38).[4] Clement uses this metaphor to contrast Christian worship and rituals with their opposite, pagan forms. Though Greek myth spoke of Orpheus, who would tame wild animals with his music, Jesus tames the wildest of animals, sinful humans. Clement writes: "See how mighty is the new song! It has made men out of stones and men out of wild beasts."[5] Christ's new song is powerful and always has been. Because David sang prophetically of this new song, his music frightened away harmful spirits (1 Sam. 16:23). Clement continues to argue that Jesus, the Word through whom all things were made (John 1:3), also "composed the entire creation into melodious order, and tuned into concert the discord of the elements, that the whole universe might be in harmony with it."[6] The Word is therefore not only the content of the "new song" but the secret of the original "pure song," who

3. Tolkien, "The Music of the Ainur," 17. For more on this material, see Jonathan McIntosh, *The Flame Imperishable: Tolkien, St. Thomas, and the Metaphysics of Faërie* (Angelico, 2017), 119–56. In *The Magician's Nephew*, C. S. Lewis also uses the metaphor of "song" to describe the creation of Narnia. His "space trilogy" is shot through with the metaphor as well.

4. Clement of Alexandria, *Exhortation to the Greeks* 1.3 (trans. G. W. Butterworth, LCL 92:7). See here Doru Costache, *Humankind and the Cosmos: Early Christian Representations* (Brill, 2021), 81–96.

5. Clement of Alexandria, *Exhortation to the Greeks* 1.5 (Butterworth, LCL 92:11).

6. Clement of Alexandria, *Exhortation to the Greeks* 1.5 (Butterworth, LCL 92:11).

created all things "in accordance with the fatherly purpose of God."[7] Clement understands that God's works, from the beginning of all things to their consummation, have a musical quality: The "new song" of redemption presupposes the "pure song" of creation, both of which are centered on the Word, the Son, Jesus Christ.

Clement's use of the "song" metaphor follows Scripture's lead, if we pay careful attention. In John's vision of heavenly worship in the book of Revelation, the angels sing a "new song" about the mystery of Christ's work:

> Worthy are you to take the scroll
>   and to open its seals,
> for you were slain, and by your blood you ransomed
>   people for God
>   from every tribe and language and people and nation,
> and you have made them a kingdom and priests to
>   our God,
>   and they shall reign on the earth. (Rev. 5:9–10; cf. 14:3)

This angelic song recalls a theme throughout the Psalms, where Israel is summoned to sing a "new song" of thanksgiving for something God has done, such as rescuing his people or intervening to bring about a new state of affairs.[8] Whenever God's people sing a "new song," they're singing of God's mighty works on their behalf. And importantly, they're singing about things that anticipate the future fulfillment of God's promises. Therefore, such new songs anticipate Christ, in whom all God's promises are "Yes and Amen" (2 Cor. 1:20).

While this theme of a "new song" throughout Scripture looks forward to the fulfillment of God's promises, it also looks

7. Clement of Alexandria, *Exhortation to the Greeks* 1.5 (Butterworth, LCL 92:13).
8. Pss. 33:3; 40:3; 96:1; 98:1; 144:9; cf. Isa. 42:10.

backward to God's mighty works in the past, the first of which is creation. In Revelation, the angels sing their "new song" against the background of a song that praises God's work of creation:

> Worthy are you, our Lord and God,
> to receive glory and honor and power,
> for you created all things,
> and by your will they existed and were created.
> (Rev. 4:11; cf. Job 38:7)

The new song about redemption follows the first song about creation. Indeed, what makes the new song "new" is the new creation Christ inaugurates: "Behold, I am making all things new" (Rev. 21:5); "if anyone is in Christ, he is a new creation" (2 Cor. 5:17; cf. Gal. 6:15). Just as the new creation presupposes the original creation, the new song presupposes an original one.

It is no minor detail that the angels sing these songs in heaven in response to God's mighty works. Notice how their song is *responsive*, much like a liturgical chant. And in many Christian churches, liturgical chants respond to chants. So Christian tradition has a place for understanding God's act of creating to be songlike, since it elicits responsive acts of singing. Of course, this is all metaphor, and it doesn't line up with Tolkien's account in every detail—he would not have wanted it so and neither do we. But metaphors help shape our imagination and understanding of things.[9] As we will see throughout our study, the metaphor of "song" is not only biblical but also, for that very reason, uniquely suited to help us understand the world, ourselves, and all that's around us as God's creation.

---

9. As helpful as metaphors are, they also crumble when pressed too far. They work best when shouldered with light burdens. Such are the burdens placed on the musical metaphors here, especially given the author's ignorance of music theory's intricacies and language. If readers fear they know too little about music, they are in good company with the author and need only press forward. If readers fear they know too much about music to forebear the book's loose metaphors, they need only a little patience and humor.

Creation is sung reality, full of beauty that can be experienced when its harmonies and resolutions are heard. But it has strange notes in it as well. Adam was born into a world of fallen angels, whose chaos intruded into Eden's peace. And creation has stranger notes still. A new song has emerged within the original, drawing it all into one grand symphony whose final movement has not yet finished. Choirs of angels, humans, and other creatures hymn the Creator's glory and wait for his music to bring everything to its rest. The glory and the weight of created life is whether we will wager our voices against the Creator or respond to his song with eternal harmonies.

The Plan of This Book

The doctrine of creation is thoroughly doxological—that is, concerned with worship. With these truths, Scripture teaches us to understand why we praise God as the Creator. The doctrine of creation is therefore about God at every point. And its end is to nourish our worship of God so that we can join the angels as they extol the Creator's glory (Rev. 4:11). Our focus on creation as God's song gives the following chapters their focus, but also some of their limitations. A fuller doctrine of creation would have to consider much more than we can in this book, such as extended treatments of the human person, sin, the natures of angels and demons, heaven and hell and the whole of a theological cosmology, and even the meaning Scripture attaches to created things like rocks, water, and fire. My treatment here is rather more modest, touching on many of these themes but leaving much unsaid. It is meant to teach as much as excite further study.

We begin by looking at the doxological framework for creation in Scripture, before moving on to consider the doctrine within this framework. Hence, the chapters proceed in order by looking at God and then his works, which includes the purpose of creation, the act of creation, the character of creatures, their variety and order, how God accomplishes all his purposes in creation, and the implications this has for life in God's cosmic household.

Bonaventure likens creation to "a kind of beautiful song" because the creation week is like music, taking time and making rhythm.[10] I will argue something similar in chapter 1 by listening to the creation week in Genesis as if it were a hymn, with defined rhythm and form. Chapter 2 looks at the presupposition of creation as a song, which is the Creator's own musicality. Here we explore the fit between the doctrine of the Trinity and the doctrine of creation, and how this helps us understand creation's contingency and its ultimate goal or end. Chapter 3 continues to look directly at the act of "singing" itself, using this as the occasion to unfold the doctrine of creation "out of nothing" (*ex nihilo*) and its consequences for how we think about creatures. Chapter 4 then turns to the theme of Jesus, God's Word, as creation's melody and the judge of its harmony. This provides us a means to revisit the creation hymn and understand deeper truths about creatures and the created order itself.

Chapter 5 considers creation's "orchestra" of creatures, who are meant to respond to God's singing liturgically, with music of their own. We also explore how this orchestra has suffered disorder because of its human conductors, who turned away from God's Word. Humanity left the song in disarray, needing resolution. When Augustine describes the world as being "like the most beautiful poem, with antitheses of a sort," he points to how aspects of creation's harmony confuse us in this life and await resolution, even though God knows the song from

10. Bonaventure, *Commentaria in quoatuor libros sententiarum magistri Petri Lombardi* II d. 13, a. 1, qa. 2, ad 2, in *Doctoris seraphici, Opera omnia* (Quaracchi, 1882), 2:316.

beginning to end.[11] Along these lines, chapter 6 looks at how Jesus resolves the creation's tensions. He is at once the fullest revelation and fulfillment of creation's doxological rhythm and form. Jesus is the song's melody become incarnate as the symphony's chief conductor, leading those who respond to God's song with music of their own. Where human conductors have failed, Christ has succeeded and freed the creation through his church to make music before the Lord. Finally, chapter 7 looks at how God's priestly image bearers should conduct the liturgy of creation. This leads us to consider our relation to other creatures and to created goods doxologically, and thus under the categories of gratitude and sacrifice—a misunderstood concept that is at the very heart of what it means to be a creature.

The "coda" is a fresh translation of Psalm 148 that showcases its poetry and musicality, and so highlights Scripture's own teaching about the nature of God's creation. I encourage you to meditate on this psalm steadily, perhaps together with Psalm 104, as you consider the claims of this book.

With all of that said, this work leaves aside questions about which some readers will no doubt expect guidance and which frequently commandeer evangelical accounts of creation. For example, we will not discuss the age of the earth. There is a very simple explanation for this: Scripture is silent on the matter. Indeed, one of this book's arguments is that Scripture shows no express interest in teaching physical cosmology. Its teaching about God and creation has metaphysical consequences for how we receive the findings of physics and biology, ruling out all sorts of false views of God's relation to the world (like deism and pantheism) and of the material cosmos itself (like naturalism and materialism). But Scripture cannot be treated like a science textbook encrypted with prescientific language and

11. Augustine, *The City of God* 11.18 (trans. William Babcock, *WSA* I/7:17).

categories. Its cosmological language is instead richly symbolic, using pictures to teach us a theological cosmology that reaches higher and deeper than any scientific account can. Readers may judge for themselves whether they are persuaded by this argument, but nothing in the book commits readers to any specific scientific account of origins, even as it rules out many ways such accounts are framed and excludes others along the way.

There are occasions in Christian theology where scientific or natural-philosophical matters should or must be dealt with in more detail, as in Christian anthropology. But the history of Christian accommodation of prevailing scientific theories of the cosmos (and even the human person) is often unflattering. That said, Christian theology is not unique in this shortcoming.[12] For instance, the older geocentric view of the cosmos was widely accepted and taught by more than simply Christians (as were infelicitous views of female dignity). Nevertheless, Christian theologians particularly erred when they mistakenly conflated these dominant views with Scripture's teaching. This conflation made them slow to accept the heliocentric model of the cosmos in the sixteenth and seventeenth centuries, despite its superior mathematical and observational virtues (not to mention its truth). To be sure, others were slow to accept these same findings. But many theologians cited Scripture in defense of geocentrism. In this, they were simply wrong on exegetical grounds, which raises the whole question of whether we should go looking for "science" and physical cosmology in Scripture at all. Perhaps there are more lessons here for us than we have learned. We will touch on these issues briefly toward the end of chapter 1, but only briefly. The book is a short introduction and more important matters merit our attention, matters that

12. See the (schematic) comments by Herman Bavinck, *Reformed Dogmatics*, ed. John Bolt, trans. John Vriend, vol. 2, *God and Creation* (Baker Academic, 2004), 484.

are rarely, if ever, present in typical presentations of this doctrine. When we are committed to the truth of Scripture, neither authors nor readers need fear being wrong. For when someone shows us a better way of understanding Scripture, we both are led by the Spirit into the truth greater than us all.

Two final notes: (1) The footnotes are for those who need them, so if that's not you, ignore them with a clean conscience. (2) The first two chapters are perhaps the most demanding. Readers who find themselves lost at moments are encouraged to keep moving, since the book is designed somewhat like a song; themes from earlier chapters reappear in later chapters that call back to them, where they are developed and expanded.

1

The Song's Doxological Nature

The Creation Hymn

Scripture opens with God creating the heavens and the earth in six days and resting on the seventh (Gen. 1:1–2:4). This is an appropriate overture, since creation is the first of God's works and sets the stage for God's covenant fellowship with his people. Christian tradition has often explored the doctrine of creation through extended commentary on the creation week, the garden of Eden, and the fall from grace.[1] In this, theologians follow Scripture's lead, since creation texts often look back to the hexaemeron (Greek for "six-day account") and echo its themes. What takes place in this week is the first word on the doctrine of creation, though it isn't the last.

1. Helpful background to the interpretation of Gen. 1 may be found in Paul M. Blowers, *The Drama of the Divine Economy: Creator and Creation in Early Christian Theology and Piety* (Oxford University Press, 2012), 101–38; Andrew J. Brown, *Recruiting the Ancients for the Creation Debate* (Eerdmans, 2023).

While the opening pages of Scripture are important historically and theologically for the doctrine of creation, they aren't alone. One might as easily unpack the doctrine of creation from Psalm 104 as from Genesis, for instance. Since the doctrine of creation arises from a comprehensive reading of Scripture, not one or two chapters, we cannot restrict our attention to any single passage. On its own, after all, Genesis is insufficient to teach us about creation. Because Jesus Christ gives us all of Scripture, only when all of it is taken together do we receive "as much as he judged sufficient."[2] We may nevertheless focus on a part of Scripture, such as the hexaemeron, so long as we relate it to the whole. That said, our first task in this initial chapter is to see how the hexaemeron is like a hymn that announces creation's doxological nature and elicits our participation. This will orient our study in the following chapters as we consider the Creator, his creative act, and his creatures from within Scripture's doxological framework.

Listening to the Hexaemeron as a Hymn

As soon as we turn to the hexaemeron, we must make some decisions about interpretation. Given the amount of attention the opening chapters of Genesis have received, there are many different views on how the text should be read and the meaning of its details.[3] It presents too many problems for almost every reader. Why is it silent about the creation of angels? Why does it speak about waters "above" the sky on day 2? Why does it speak of days, of morning and evening, before the creation of the sun and moon? And so on. The one unspoken assumption

2. Augustine, *City of God* 11.3 (trans. William Babcock, *WSA* I/7:3).

3. For a concise introduction to such debates, see Daniel J. Treier, *Introducing Evangelical Theology* (Baker Academic, 2019), 138–46. The careful and charitable reader will notice that the current chapter's argument doesn't necessarily exclude any party in these debates.

almost all interpreters of the hexaemeron share is that this is not the text they would've written.

Good! For this very reason, it keeps us on our toes. Scripture resists every narrow interest, every tidy attempt to bottle it up. There are no good answers to bad questions, and the questions that the answers from Scripture presuppose are not always the ones we initially think to ask. Vigilant against the temptation of clinging to the wrong questions, we must therefore question our questions to see whether they are the right ones.

That said, it's not easy to discern when one's questions are wrong and when they're right. How can we be certain we've captured the right sense of the text? Martin Luther held to what he considered a commonsense approach to the text, for he believed that Scripture's meaning is found in "the simplest language" of its literal sense.[4] Despite its simple language, however, Luther admitted that the hexaemeron is a difficult text to interpret, so no one theologian is a safe guide to all its particulars.[5] This is a sage warning: On his own, neither Luther nor Basil nor Augustine nor any other interpreter (the present author included) is a sufficient guide to the whole text. The safest approach to this text, like any other, is to look at it from several angles and with several other interpreters past and present. Such is the approach I will take in this chapter.

In this light, careful interpretation requires at least two things of us. First, we must approach the hexaemeron with a teachable spirit. Christian tradition has long recognized that the most decisive feature of the hexaemeron is that it is prophetic speech: God instructing us through his prophet of things we need to know for

4. Martin Luther, *Lectures on Genesis*, chaps. 1–5 (*LW* 1:3). While Luther is right about the simple language of the literal sense, there are good biblical and theological reasons to disagree that he consistently identified the meaning of this language in the hexaemeron.

5. Luther, *Lectures on Genesis*, chaps. 1–5 (*LW* 1:4).

our salvation. It might sound strange to call this text prophecy, but we simply mean that it's something God had to teach "Moses, the scribe of truth."[6] The prophets declare the oracles of God. Prophets do not spend their time satisfying idle curiosities or lecturing on things like physics and biology. The text before us aims at our sanctification. So we must receive it with humility, teachability, and love of God. If our interpretation does not summon these virtues into action and make claims on our lives, we have good reason to question whether we've received God's prophetic speech.

Second, this teachability requires that we attend expectantly, repentantly, and diligently to the text's details and form. Any viable reading must do justice to the creation week's obvious and painstaking literary structure. Typically, this involves questions about the "genre" of the hexaemeron: Is it historical narrative, wisdom literature, "myth," poetry, or something else besides? As most interpreters will agree, the genre is hard to pigeonhole. It shares common features with poetry and with prose, having repetition, silences, and exacting organization, but also a narrative sequence that departs from traditional Hebrew poetry such as one often finds in the Psalms. The hexaemeron is perhaps closer to what we often call prose poetry. Like the function of rhyme in a poem, the days point backward and forward, suspending the march of time to awaken something timeless in the reader.[7] And like sequence in a narrative, the days build upon one another and lead to a climax.

We can capture all this by likening the hexaemeron to a hymn. Indeed, with Luther we can affirm that Scripture's meaning is found in its simple language. But what language is sim-

6. Jacob of Serug, *Homily on the Fashioning of Creation*, trans. Edward G. Mathews Jr., Texts from Christian Antiquity 67 (Gorgias, 2021), 57–58; cf. Basil of Caesarea, *Homilies on the Hexaemeron* 1.1 (FC 46:4–5).

7. On the function of rhyme in this way, see Brad Leithauser, *Rhyme's Rooms: The Architecture of Poetry* (Knopf, 2022), 138.

pler for teaching little ones than the language of song? With its structure, rhythm, and movement, the hexaemeron works like a hymn to teach us about the orderly work of the Creator in a heavily stylized and memorable form. Much like a hymn, then, the hexaemeron at once praises the Creator and invites the church to join in this praise. In what follows, we will therefore listen to the hexaemeron as a hymn, to perceive its poetic images and feel its rhythm—and to be taught like children.

The Hymn's Doxological Rhythm and Order

The hexaemeron appears like a hymn when we pay attention to two patterns in the text, which concern time and space—two of created life's most inescapable realities.[8] Both patterns follow clear structures within the text and discern its meaning, while neither on its own exhausts all there is to say. We can understand this if we liken the temporal pattern to the hymn's rhythm and the spatial pattern to the hymn's order. If we only listened to a song's rhythm, we would miss much of what makes the song a coherent piece of music. And without listening to a song's rhythm, we could not join it with our voices or instruments. Looking at both aspects will help us understand creation's context in doxology, worship. We must therefore consider (1) the hymn's temporal pattern as its doxological rhythm and (2) its spatial pattern as its doxological order.

The Hymn's Temporal Pattern, Creation's Doxological Rhythm

Arguably, the main progression of the creation week is concerned with time. This is evident in each of the six days, which

8. Ben C. Ollenburger, *God the Creator: The Old Testament and the World God Is Making* (Baker Academic, 2023), 20–25, discusses the "liturgical" and "spatial" patterns in the hexaemeron. See also L. Michael Morales, *Who Shall Ascend the Mountain of the Lord? A Biblical Theology of the Book of Leviticus*, NSBT 37 (IVP Academic, 2015), 39–49.

are like verses in a song, all (except for the seventh) ending with the refrain "there was evening and there was morning, the [*n*th] day" (Gen. 1:5, 8, 13, 19, 23, 31). However, it's especially prominent in the verses sounded at the beginning, the middle, and the end, in the progression from the first to the fourth and seventh days (fig. 1). These three days all share a common theme as well as a common rhythm.

Day 1		Light (sign of God's glory)
	Day 2	
	Day 3	
Day 4		Sun, Moon, and Stars (symbols of God's glorious presence in worship)
	Day 5	
	Day 6	
Day 7		Rest and Perpetual Light (freedom for worship, to glorify God)

Figure 1. Temporal pattern

Like a theme developed in a song, the temporal pattern develops the theme of time within the framework of God's glory and creation's doxological purpose. This is why we hear notes of "light" in these days and why they conclude in worship. Throughout Scripture, light is often a metaphor of God's glory (Isa. 60:1; John 1:9–14; 2 Cor. 4:6), an association that the creation hymn subtly supports. Light arrives on the first day without any physical source. This curious fact grabs our attention and focuses it on God, who is light's ultimate source, and not on the heavenly bodies (sun, moon, stars). Light points beyond itself to God: he is robed "with light" (Ps. 104:2); he "dwells in unapproachable light" (1 Tim. 6:16); and finally, he "is light"

(1 John 1:5). God speaks and light shines in the darkness, for God's Word is enlightening light (John 1:9; cf. 1 John 2:8). This Word is the Lamb, who will be the only source of light in the new heavens and new earth: "And the city has no need of sun or moon to shine on it, for the glory of God gives it light, and its lamp is the Lamb" (Rev. 21:23; cf. Isa. 60:19).

Light on day 1 thus foreshadows God's glorious presence. At the center of this temporal pattern is the fourth day with the heavenly bodies, which are deputized to "rule" the passing of time (Gen. 1:16). These lights are described with the same word used across the Pentateuch for the lamps in the tabernacle, which represent God's presence and provision (Ex. 25:30–31; 35:8, 14, 28; 40:4; Num. 8:1–4; 1 Kings 7:49; Rev. 11:4). Like the tabernacle's lamps, then, the "lamps" mediating heavenly light are reminders of the light of God's countenance that shines upon his people when they gather to worship him (Num. 6:24–26; cf. 2 Cor. 4:6). The seventh day, with its mysterious absence of evening and morning, paints a picture of light enduring without these lamps. Again, in John's vision of the new creation and the saints' worship of the Lamb, we read that "night will be no more. They will need no light of lamp or sun, for the Lord God will be their light, and they will reign forever and ever" (Rev. 22:5). Light appears on the horizon of time, followed by the heavenly bodies that run their course, and when they are finished, the light of God's glory will remain forevermore. All this imagery shows us that time itself revolves around the glory of God.

While these three days develop the common theme of light pointing to God's glory, they also share a common rhythm. Just as time is characterized by its movement from and to God's glory, so it exists to facilitate Israel's worship. Time has a doxological rhythm. This emphasis on worship is explicit at the week's center. The fourth day is central to the temporal pattern, because here the heavenly bodies are introduced with their purpose: They "separate the day from the night" and function to tell of "signs and festivals, and for days and years" (Gen. 1:14).[9] God delegates created light to the heavenly bodies so that the march of time is measurable in days and years.

More importantly for the hymn's purpose, however, is how time's forward march is tethered to "festivals," Israel's seven religious feasts on which they would celebrate the gifts of their Creator and rest from their labors.[10] These harvest feasts and pilgrimages would celebrate the Creator's goodness in providing food and afford households the opportunities to compare their crops and yields, identifying people who were in need, and share their bounty accordingly. They would remind Israel that the Creator owns his creation, so the gifts of its fruitfulness should be shared with "the poor and the sojourner" rather than hoarded by the cleverest and most ruthless (Lev. 23:22). But these same feasts would point also to God's rescue of Israel from sin and slavery so they might be free to worship him: "Let my people go, that they may serve me" (Ex. 8:1).

The seventh day introduces the first of these feasts, the Sabbath (Gen. 2:2; cf. Ex. 20:8–11). This day is the reason for the

9. A note on the word "festival" (*mo'adim*) is in order. The ESV translates *mo'adim* as "seasons," but the word only possibly (and very rarely) refers to the seasons of the year. Most often it refers to the "appointed time" or "fixed time" that is synonymous with the liturgical feasts (cf. Lev. 23). See Walter Vogels, "The Cultic and Civil Calendars of the Fourth Day of Creation (Gen. 1:14b)," *Scandinavian Journal of the Old Testament* 11, no. 2 (1997): 163–66. Following Vogels, I have used "festivals" as the clearest translation of the word's meaning in context.

10. The seven annual feasts were Passover (Lev. 23:5), Unleavened Bread (Lev. 23:6–8), Firstfruits (Lev. 23:9–14), Weeks (Lev. 23:15–22), Trumpets (Lev. 23:23–25), Day of Atonement (Lev. 23:26–32), and Booths (Lev. 23:33–44). For a helpful overview of the agrarian function of these feasts, see Michael LeFebvre, *The Liturgy of Creation: Understanding Calendars in Old Testament Context* (IVP Academic, 2019), 38–53, who also reads the hexaemeron as a liturgical calendar in ways suggestive for my approach in this chapter. On the evolution of feasts in early Christianity, see Paul F. Bradshaw and Maxwell E. Johnson, *The Origins of Feasts, Fasts, and Seasons in Early Christianity* (Liturgical Press, 2011).

numbering of the creation week's days in the first place, tying them together into a collective portrait: a miniature liturgical calendar that gathers up the whole cosmos and sets its daily, weekly, monthly, and yearly rhythms, thereby leading it into the blessing of God's presence. It is the Sabbath that unifies the other days, since they count down to it. So, too, Israel's festal calendar counts from one feast to the next (cf. Lev. 23), and the years count to the year of jubilee, in which all things are given rest and a new beginning (Lev. 25:8–55). The Sabbath comes first in the ordering of the feasts in Leviticus 23 because it is archetypal, showing how every religious feast is rooted ultimately in the Creator's bountiful provision in creation, which looks forward to something greater (cf. Heb. 4:9–10). Like creation itself, time is for the benefit of God's creatures and their daily existence, but it also points beyond itself to the Creator and the end of time in his eternity. Creation's doxological rhythm should culminate in gratitude that shares the bounty of the Creator's generosity, and gives all God's people the rest they need to worship him.

Much like a hymn or a call to worship, creation's doxological rhythm orders and governs Israel's worship, and especially its religious calendar. By that same token, it shows how God opens time to himself so that he may meet his creatures there and have time for them. Creation is not trapped by time, so creatures don't need deliverance from it. Rather, created time is part of God's hospitality. The seventh day brings time to rest in God's rest, a sign of how time is supposed to be ordered and inhabited for the flourishing of God's creatures. "The Sabbath was made for man, not man for the Sabbath" (Mark 2:27), on account of which it is "a delight" (Isa. 58:13). When God met Israel in their annual cycle of feasts, this reminded them of his provision in and with the rhythm of created time: "While the earth remains, seedtime and harvest, cold and heat, summer and winter, day and night, shall not cease" (Gen. 8:22). Time is a fit vehicle for God's fellowship with creatures. As Israel ordered their lives by the calendar the heavenly bodies regulated, they ordered their earthly lives with the hospitable, doxological rhythm of heaven.[11] For this same reason, many churches observe a liturgical calendar that structures the year by festivals and days to remember the Creator's presence with his creatures in time.[12] Such practices embody the biblical sense that God creates time with purpose, meaning, and order, all of which invite and regulate our worship for our good.

The Hymn's Spatial Pattern, Creation's Doxological Order

Complementing the temporal pattern is the creation week's spatial pattern. This concerns how God separates spaces within creation and fills them. Broadly speaking, this is one of the most traditional ways of looking at the creation week.[13] According to this pattern, God "forms" habitats and subsequently "fills" those habitats with inhabitants. At the outset of the week, creation is "without form and void" (Gen. 1:2), hinting at a state of formlessness and emptiness. As the week progresses, God's creative

11. LeFebvre, *The Liturgy of Creation*, 24. See also Brittany N. Melton, "An Invitation to a New Era of Biblical Theology: Towards an Old Testament Theology of Hospitality," *Tyndale Bulletin* 74, no. 1 (2023): 113–41.

12. The Christian year is structured around the mysteries of Christ's life, especially his birth, passion, resurrection, and ascension. This is because Christ embraces in himself everything that the feasts of Lev. 23 point toward; he is the "body" of which the feasts were all "shadows" (Col. 2:17). Israel's liturgical feasts not only gathered the people together for worship and the celebration of God's bounty but also gathered time cyclically around the Creator. So, too, Christ "gathers" together all things in himself in the "fullness of time" (Eph. 1:10). Time is created by, through, and for Jesus Christ (Col. 1:16), being thereby structured around him (cf. Rev. 5). We return to this in chap. 6, under "Bringing It All Together," when discussing how Christ "recapitulates" all things in himself (see p. 123).

13. "Broadly speaking": While individual authors differ on what exactly is taking place in days 1–3 and days 4–6, they tend to agree in discerning a distinction and stylistic symmetry between the two sets of days. For instance, in book 2 of his *Sentences* (distinctions 12–15), Peter Lombard is representative when he classifies God's works in the six days of "distinguishing" (days 1–3) and "adorning" (days 4–6). While this classification of the six days is often associated with the so-called "framework view" in contemporary literature, we must not flatten into one monolithic perspective every individual author recognizing this symmetry.

activity remedies this barrenness with acts of "forming" and "filling." The same distinction is echoed in the week's conclusion, where "the heavens and earth were finished [formed], and all the host of them [filled]" (Gen. 2:1; cf. Isa. 45:18).[14] (See fig. 2.)

Forming		**Filling**		
Day 1 (Gen. 1:3–5)	Separates light and darkness	*Day 4* (Gen. 1:14–19)	Creates sun, moon, stars to help creatures track signs, religious festivals, days, years	*Day 7* (Gen. 2:1–3) Sanctification, rest, worship led by God's image bearers, like priests over all creation
Day 2 (Gen. 1:6–8)	Separates waters above (sky) and below (sea)	*Day 5* (Gen. 1:20–23)	Creates inhabitants of the seas and skies	
Day 3 (Gen. 1:9–13)	Separates seas from land (also brings forth vegetation from earth)	*Day 6* (Gen. 1:24–31)	Creates insects and beasts on land, but especially humanity	

Figure 2. Spatial pattern

The week's spatial pattern divides the six days into two halves, whereupon we can see correspondences between the

14. The framework of "forming" and "filling" is sometimes criticized because day 3 seems to cheat with the "forming" of land *and* the "filling" of vegetation. See, for a recent example, Joel R. Beeke and Paul M. Smalley, *Reformed Systematic Theology*, vol. 2, *Man and Christ* (Crossway, 2020), 98. However, per Henri Blocher, *In the Beginning: The Opening Chapters of Genesis* (InterVarsity Press, 1984), 52, this is a feature, not a bug of the spatial structure. Day 3 simultaneously concludes the "forming" days while also pointing forward to the "filling" days. Something parallel happens on day 6: God fills the earth with all sorts of beasts, but he also fills it with humanity. Just as the vegetation of day 3 points us forward to the following days, the image bearers on day 6 point us forward to day 7, for they are the ones invited to rest in God and lead all creation in that direction. Just as day 3 points forward to God's acts of filling as the completion of creation's forming, so day 6 points forward to God's rest as the completion of creation itself. The days of creation are linked together with a clear literary structure, weaving in and out of one another like a good poem or song.

first three days and the last three.[15] In days 1 through 3, God forms spaces by distinguishing and separating parts of the world's unformed mass. On day 1, God separates light from darkness (Gen. 1:3–5); on day 2, it's the waters above separated from the waters below, or heaven from the earth (Gen. 1:6–8); and on day 3, he separates the dry land from the waters, or earth from sea (Gen. 1:9–13). Throughout days 4–6, God respectively "fills" the spaces he previously formed by decorating or adorning them with living things. On day 4, God assigns the phases of light and darkness to the sun, moon, and stars (Gen. 1:14–19); on day 5, he fills the heavens with birds and the waters with aquatic life (Gen. 1:20–23); and on day 6, he decorates the earth with beasts and, above all, humans (Gen. 1:24–31).

One final feature of this pattern deserves comment. God pronounces his creation "good" *twice*, on days 3 and 6, which respectively conclude the days of forming and the days of filling (Gen. 1:10, 12, 25, 31). This pronouncement underscores that God's acts of forming and filling address the problem of creation's barrenness and cultivate it for fruitfulness. Day 7 is the capstone of the whole structure, sanctified and blessed as its fullness (Gen. 2:3). This climactic day and the preceding six days demarcate one week decorated with the freedom to rest and enjoy the Creator's rich bounty.

The spatial pattern of the creation week highlights the Creator's unilateral provision for the structures of life. Creation has not only rhythmic time, therefore, but "structured space."[16] This is especially visible in the important work of "distinction" or "separation." God distinguishes the elements of creation so

---

15. Each set of three days has roughly the same number of Hebrew words devoted to them (207 words in days 1–3 and 206 words in days 4–6), with the words of all six days adding up to a multiple of seven (7 x 59 = 413). See Paul Beauchamp, *Création et séparation: Étude éxegétique du chapitre premier de la Genèse* (Éditions du Cerf, 2005), 71–76.

16. Rolf P. Knierim, "Cosmos and History," in *The Task of Old Testament Theology: Substance, Method, and Cases* (Eerdmans, 1995), 186.

that they have space to function and then provides for their continued separation and working.[17] Hence, God creates light in distinction from darkness, and then he creates the luminaries to sustain and govern this separation. The sky separates the upper waters from the lower waters and thereby opens space for the flourishing of aerial and aquatic life. The sea's separation from the dry ground opens a space for the vegetation, beasts, and human life that inhabit the earth. It is crucial for the Christian vision of creation to notice that God's distinctions create space for creatures to come together in fertile and life-giving ways.[18] God's distinctions are therefore gifts of order, spaces where God meets his creation and provides for life and fruitfulness. The psalmist therefore praises the Creator's work of establishing boundaries between creation's ordered spaces (Ps. 104:9), since this is the condition for the flourishing of those spaces and their inhabitants (Ps. 104:10–15). The hymn's order thus hints at creation's order, articulated by the Creator's act of distinguishing.

On a deeper level, then, creation's order is doxological. It is the setting for how creatures, especially humans, will glorify God and display his goodness in all of life. Just as the hymn displays doxological order, so too humans are created to display this order in their lives by hearing and obeying God's word with love that is well ordered. We see this in relief against the background of how the hexaemeron's spatial pattern narrates the distinction between Creator and creation: God is prior to all the things he creates, and they are distinct from one another only as the Creator rescues them from their original disorder and sets them in order with his peace. Order is part of God imprinting likenesses of his own goodness and wisdom on creation (Ps. 148:6; Prov. 3:19; 8:22–31).

17. See here Ollenburger, *God the Creator*, 24–25.

18. Ephraim Radner, *A Time to Keep: Theology, Mortality, and the Shape of a Human Life* (Baylor University Press, 2016), 92–96.

That said, likeness to God is not identity with God. The Creator's distinction from creatures is fundamental and inescapable. As the narrative of Genesis 3–11 shows, however, the creature alienates itself from its Creator as it tries to erase these foundational distinctions and therefore tear down the unassailable difference between Creator and creature (cf. Rom. 1:25).[19] Sin manifests itself partly in the drive to neglect the Creator's act of separating: either by obliterating created distinctions, reducing creation's rich diversity to a dismal sameness, or by stretching these distinctions into alienations. Hence, creation's distinctions between spaces are echoed in the distinction between "kinds" of vegetation and animal life (Gen. 1:11–12, 21, 24–25), as well as between the two human sexes (Gen. 1:27). All these distinctions express the shape of the Creator's will, to which Israel is conformed through God's word. "What God has distinguished and created distinct, man ought not to confuse (Lev. 19:19; Deut. 22:9–11)."[20] Lawful worship in everyday life, which touches upon everything from agriculture to marriage, requires careful discernment of how God orders reality for fruitfulness through acts of distinction. Living within God's created order wisely and worshipfully is thus a matter of following the hymn's doxological order.

From Cosmos to Temple: Creation's Doxological Character

Having looked at the creation hymn's musical patterns, we must now grasp the inseparability of Scripture's form for the content of what it teaches us about creation. We will look at this in the next two sections. First, we consider its "liturgical"

19. On this collapsing of distinctions throughout the narrative, see Morales, *Who Shall Ascend?*, 51–74; Edward W. Klink III, *The Beginning and End of All Things: A Biblical Theology of Creation and New Creation*, Essential Studies in Biblical Theology (IVP Academic, 2023), 54–66.

20. Gordon Wenham, *Genesis 1–15*, Word Biblical Commentary (Thomas Nelson, 1987), 21.

form and then its "poetic" form, each of which have valuable lessons for understanding Scripture's teaching about creation.

Together, the creation week's temporal and spatial patterns converge to show us how God disposes creation to sustain creaturely life. More centrally, they teach us that creatures flourish when they organize their life around the Creator worshipfully. The creation hymn's doxological rhythm and order thus display creation's character as the place where God's glory will be manifest and celebrated. That is to say, creation structures and elicits worship of the Creator—hence its form as a sort of "liturgy."[21] As we must now see, this form gets to the very heart of the doctrine of creation's content.

"Liturgy" (from the Greek *leitourgia*) is any form of orderly, corporate religious service. It involves speech and actions structured by consecrated time and space as occasions for fellowship with God. Churches gather on Sundays because they reflect this order, and many churches name the order of their services (or parts of it) as the "liturgy." In part, liturgy reflects the church's corporate sense that they are all partaking in an act of service to God that is bigger than individual members of the church body, and especially bigger than anyone's personal preferences. Since peace is "the tranquility of order," worship should be orderly because it responds to the God of peace (1 Cor. 14:33, 40).[22] The hexaemeron offers us a liturgy of creation in at least two ways: (1) in its shape as a hymn and (2) in its temple imagery.

The Hexaemeron's Shape as a Hymn

First of all, liturgical interests saturate the hexaemeron's form as poetic hymn. In the most significant places where Scripture

21. Representatively, see Samuel E. Balentine, *The Torah's Vision of Worship* (Fortress, 1999), 81–95.

22. Augustine, *City of God* 19.13 (Babcock, *WSA* I/7:368). A similar vision animates Gregory of Nazianzus's *Oration* 6.

teaches about creation, it does so in the context of praise and doxology. Examples abound:

> Let all the earth fear the Lord;
> let all the inhabitants of the world stand in awe of him!
> For he spoke, and it came to be;
> he commanded, and it stood firm. (Ps. 33:8–9)

> O Lord, how manifold are your works!
> In wisdom you have made them all;
> the earth is full of your creatures. (Ps. 104:24)

> Worthy are you, our Lord and God,
> to receive glory and honor and power,
> for you created all things,
> and by your will they existed and were created. (Rev. 4:11)

Even Paul's statement about creation taking place through and for Christ is in the form of a hymn (Col. 1:15–20).

The creation week is not much different in this regard. Before there is a congregation to respond to, God utters his own Word and its response—which is to say, before there is any choir, the conductor raises his own voice. Space for creaturely response arrives in the climax of all the other days, the seventh, which God sanctifies and blesses as the model for enjoying his creation's fruitfulness and for returning it to him in praise. When creation was completed,

> the morning stars sang together
> and all the sons of God shouted for joy. (Job 38:7)

The liturgical response of the stars and angels is a model for our own. All creatures are summoned to praise the Creator, beginning with angels, the sun and moon, the waters and mountains and others, leading all the way finally to humans (cf. Ps. 148). Hence, God brings about a "sung world—a song not only sung, but a song giving rise to new singers."[23]

As a song or a hymn, the hexaemeron invites its readers to confess the Creator's majesty, order their lives by creation's doxological rhythm and order, and praise God for his mighty works. We find this in the great psalm of creation, which begins with confession:

> O Lord my God, you are very great!
> You are clothed with splendor and majesty. (Ps. 104:1)

This leads into a hymn of creation's order and artistry, concluding with a vision of creation inhabited only by those who praise God:

> I will sing to the Lord as long as I live;
> I will sing praise to my God while I have being. . . .
> Let sinners be consumed from the earth,
> and the let the wicked be no more! (Ps. 104:33, 35)

The reminder that the "way of the wicked will perish" (Ps. 1:6) restates that sin was not part of God's created order and has no proper place within it. The Creator's song began without dissonance and will end in pure harmony, when it blends with the "new song" that completes the first: the song of the Lamb slain to reclaim his creation in all its resonance (Rev. 5:11–13; 14:3).

The Hexaemeron's Temple Imagery

Second, the hexaemeron uses imagery that is evocative of the temple, where Israel would gather to worship God in his

23. William Desmond, *God and the Between* (Blackwell, 2008), 253.

presence. Attuning our ears to the hymn's rhythm and imagery, we discover that the stories of creation and the construction of the tabernacle strike several common notes. For instance, in each account the "Spirit of God," full of wisdom and knowledge, is present and active before the work begins.[24] More importantly for creation's doxological character, the number seven and its association with the climax of the hexaemeron loom large. Before Moses receives instructions for the tabernacle, he waits for six days until the Lord finally appears on the seventh (Ex. 24:16). As in the hexaemeron, there are seven commands and acts of response in which God issues a command and then it is done.[25] Later in Leviticus, instructions for sacrificial activities are reported in seven speeches, and rituals such as the ordination of priests last for seven days (Lev. 1–7; 8:33).[26] Each account includes signal acts of beholding, completing, blessing, and sanctifying the work, and each notably concludes with Sabbath rest.[27]

Many of these parallels between creation and the tabernacle or temple are allusive and gather their force cumulatively.[28] Just as God stretches out the heavens like a tent, so Israel makes "curtains of goats' hair for a tent over the tabernacle" (Ex. 26:7; Ps. 104:2). God makes the "firmament" to separate the waters from one another, and Israel hangs a veil to "separate" the "Holy Place from the Most Holy" (Gen. 1:6–8; Ex. 26:33). Corresponding to the waters under the firmament on day 2 is the bronze basin filled with water, in which the priests wash their hands and feet before approaching the altar or entering the

24. Gen. 1:2; Ex. 31:3, 35:31; cf. Prov. 3:19–20.

25. Gen. 1:3, 6, 9, 14, 20, 24, 26; Ex. 25:1; 30:11, 17, 22, 34; 31:1, 12.

26. Balentine, *The Torah's Vision of Worship*, 64.

27. Acts: Gen. 1:21; 2:1–3; Ex. 39:32, 43; 40:9–11, 33–34. Rest: Gen. 2:2–3; Ex. 31:12–17.

28. For all the correspondences that follow and more, see the collection of essays *Cult and Cosmos: Tilting Toward a Temple-Centered Theology*, ed. L. Michael Morales, Biblical Tools and Studies 14 (Peeters, 2014).

tabernacle (Gen. 1:7; Ex. 30:17–21). There are "lamps" in the heavens and lampstands in the tabernacle (Gen. 1:14–15; Ex. 25:31–40), birds flying across the heavens and winged cherubim spread across the mercy seat (Gen. 1:20; Ex. 25:20). As there are priests to lead in the tabernacle's liturgy, so there are Adam and Eve to lead creation's liturgy (Gen. 1:27; Ex. 28:1). Acts of "separating" also draw an analogy between the creation and the liturgy around the tabernacle.[29] And in imitation of God finishing his work and blessing it, Israel finishes the tabernacle's construction and Moses blesses it (Gen. 2:1–3; Ex. 39:32, 43). These allusions fuel an analogy between creation and the temple, for which reason creation is compared to a tabernacle (Job 9:8; Ps. 104:2; Isa. 40:22; 66:1–2), or a house in which the heavens, supported by pillars (Job 26:11), have windows and doors (Gen. 7:11; Ps. 78:23). This is perhaps nowhere more explicit than in John's vision of the new heavens and the new earth as a garden-like city functioning like the temple (Rev. 21–22).

While these parallels strongly point to creation's doxological character, many of them fall short of strict one-to-one comparisons, so we should not equate creation and the temple. The temple is *like* a small cosmos; and the world, *like* a cosmic sanctuary (Ps. 78:69). The analogy between the two highlights a similarity within a dissimilarity. The creation bends toward the temple; the temple shows what the creation will become: a place where God's glory resounds with reasonable praise. God intends that the temple's sacred space expand to include the whole cosmos.[30] Creation is not that yet; but, Jesus reminds us, "My Father is

29. Separating in creation: Gen. 1:4, 6, 7, 14, 18. Separating in liturgy: Ex. 26:33; Lev. 1:17; 5:8; 10:10; 11:47; 20:24–26; Num. 8:14; 16:9. See G. Geoffrey Harper, *"I Will Walk Among You": The Rhetorical Function of Allusion to Genesis 1–3 in the Book of Leviticus* (Eisenbrauns, 2018), 128.

30. G. K. Beale and Mitchell Kim, *God Dwells Among Us: Expanding Eden to the Ends of the Earth* (IVP Academic, 2021).

working until now, and I am working" (John 5:17). One way we see the importance of registering the difference between creation and the temple is in the distinction between God's "rest" on the seventh day (Gen. 2:2) and God's "rest" upon entering the temple (Ex. 20:11; Ps. 132:8). They are closely related but nonetheless distinct. The latter rest is tied to Israel's God-given rest from their enemies.[31] But of course, there are no enemies from whom God would need rest on the seventh day of creation. The point of comparison between the two is that they both are related to God's peace, which he grants to creation in the beginning and will secure indestructibly in the end. The movement from cosmos to temple moves from one participation in God's peace to another, and the vehicle of this movement is God's covenant. Creation is, from the beginning, built for worship, and it will be consummated in worship. Its character is doxological.

The Importance of Poetry and Symbolism for the Doctrine of Creation

As we have just seen, Scripture routinely teaches us about creation in the form of liturgical texts and liturgical figures, such as the temple. This is not accidental but intrinsic to the lesson we are taught: Creation has a doxological nature. Now we must make a second, complementary observation, which is that Scripture also routinely employs poetry and symbolism when teaching us about creation. In different ways, Scripture is like a book with pictures, using its own form of iconography to teach us larger truths. Literary forms like poetry and hymns employ a rich array of symbolism and metaphor to make their observations, and to make them memorable. What does this form of Scripture's teaching tell us about the contents of creation? Why not rather just narrate creation to us in the form of a chronol-

31. 2 Sam. 7:1; cf. Deut. 12:9; 1 Kings 5:3–4; 8:56.

ogy, or tell it to us like the modern sciences do, in the form of a physical cosmology?

First, we should recognize that Scripture employs poetic language extensively when talking about creation. For a few examples: God "treads on the heights of the earth" (Amos 4:13); he is the one

> who builds his upper chambers in the heavens
>   and founds his vault upon the earth;
> who calls for the waters of the sea
>   and pours them out upon the surface of the earth.
>   (Amos 9:6)

God weighs the mountains in scales and collects coastlands in his hand like a fistful of sand (Isa. 40:12, 15); he bottles up the seas in their places with sands (Jer. 5:22); he delivers the sea like a newborn and wraps it in darkness like swaddling clothes (Job 38:8–9); he makes the clouds rain as if he's tilting heavenly "waterskins" (Job 38:37). And then there are several places where Scripture personifies the sea and the unformed and unfilled state of creation, likening them poetically to mythical dragons and monsters God has conquered (Job 26:12; Pss. 74:13–17; 89:9–10). Such places recall how Scripture elsewhere personifies creation with human affections and agency.[32]

Poetic symbolism can easily escape notice or be misinterpreted—it often is. But it bears on what the Spirit is teaching us when he instructs us about creation. Consider the great creation psalm again, where God is "stretching out the heavens like a tent" (Ps. 104:2) and has

> set the earth on its foundations,
>   so that it should never be moved. (Ps. 104:5)

32. Pss. 19:1; 50:6; 65:12–13; 148; Rom. 8:19–22.

It would be a mistake to read this as "primitive" blundering about the physical cosmos before the dawn of modern science. This vivid imagery of the heavens as a tent covering, or the earth rooted on foundations "like a giant oil-rig set up in the midst of the oceans," shows us rather that "poetry is the proper language of creation."[33] There may be many reasons for this, some known only to God's infinite wisdom. But two reasons stand out: (1) poetry can speak to truths like "order" that mere narrative reports threaten to obstruct; and (2) poetry can disclose these truths while also preserving the mystery of creation and its order.

Poetry Teaches Order and Meaning

Poetic language and forms are more transparent for teaching us about creation's order than would be a mere chronology, like a news report that carefully relays a timeline of events, or a physical cosmology conveying information about physics and biology.[34] Whereas chronological or scientific reports primarily consist of descriptive facts, poetry communicates order, meaning, and significance. It tells us about truths that transcend history and narrative, truths that shape history. Such is the truth about creation, since creation is the presupposition of everything that happens in history. The hymn of creation tells us more about the beginning of time and space than about what happens within time and space.[35] It instructs us about how time

33. Patrick D. Miller, "The Poetry of Creation: Psalm 104," in *The Way of The Lord: Essays in Old Testament Theology* (Eerdmans, 2007), 185. For companionable reflections on Gen. 1–2, see Ellen Davis, *Scripture, Culture, and Agriculture: An Agrarian Reading of the Bible* (Cambridge University Press, 2009), 42–65.

34. In this connection, compare the critical comments on historicism in Oliver O'Donovan, *Resurrection and Moral Order: An Outline for Evangelical Ethics*, 2nd ed. (Eerdmans, 1994), 60–63.

35. Scripture's narration of events within time and space begins after the creation hymn. Right after God's seventh-day rest, Scripture announces, "These are the generations / of the heavens and the earth when they were created, / in the day that the Lord God made the earth and the heavens" (Gen. 2:4). This is the first in a series of important

and space are ordered for the praise of God, and thus how we should steward these aspects of our existence.

Throughout the Old Testament, the literary structure of prayers, songs, and poetry conveys their authors' inspired perception of creation's order.[36] We will return to creation's order in later chapters. But first we must register that when Scripture's stock of symbolism and metaphors is properly understood, it's very difficult to maintain that it misleads us with pseudoscience. Scripture does not teach that the earth is flat, that the sky is a solid structure standing on top of it like a bell jar, or that God somehow lives "up" in the sky.[37] Biblical cosmology should not be mistaken for a scientific riddle, or a childlike, prescientific understanding of the world—that way lies the confusion of prophetic discourse with the discourse of modern physics. Nor does Scripture's poetic personification of creation teach that,

---

"generations" sayings ("these are the generations of x, y, z.") that structure the book of Genesis, signaling important moments in the history of God's covenant fellowship with his people. Sometimes these "generations" sayings will introduce a genealogy (Gen. 5:1; 10:1; 11:10, etc.), while at other times they introduce a narrative (Gen. 2:4; 6:9; 11:27; etc.). In both cases, however, the phrase "generations of x, y, z" points to something that arises from what has preceded. The word for "generations" is associated with the word for "birth." Therefore, according to Raymond C. Van Leeuwen, "Creation and Contingency in Qoheleth," in *The Identity of Israel's God in Christian Scripture*, ed. Don Collett, Mark Elliott, Mark Gignilliat, and Ephraim Radner (SBL, 2020), 149n19, these sayings communicate something like, "this situation or person was born out of the preceding situation or persons." See, further, Sarah Schwartz, "Narrative *Toledot* Formulae in Genesis: The Case of Heaven and Earth, Noah, and Isaac," *Journal of Hebrew Scriptures* 16, no. 8 (2016): 1–36; Don C. Collett, *Figural Reading and the Old Testament: Theology and Practice* (Baker Academic, 2020), 9–23; Jean-Pierre Sonnet, "Generare, perché? Una prospettiva biblica," *Anthropotes* 36 (2020): 139–90.

36. Cf. Knierim, "Cosmos and History," 186–87.

37. Among others, see Othmar Keel and Silvia Schroer, *Creation: Biblical Theologies in the Context of the Ancient Near East*, trans. Peter T. Daniels (Eisenbrauns, 2015), 78–79; Bernd Janowski, "Das biblische Weltbild: Eine methodologische Skizze," in *Das biblische Weltbild und seine altorientalischen Kontext*, ed. Bernd Janowski and Beate Ego. Forschungen zum Alten Testament 32 (Mohr Siebeck, 2001), 3–26. As will be clear to readers of these other sources, the argument here presses some of their insights further in a figural direction. The New Testament is similar to the Old in this regard. According to Sean M. McDonough and Jonathan T. Pennington, "Conclusion," in *Cosmology and New Testament Theology*, ed. Sean M. McDonough and Jonathan T. Pennington, LNTS 355 (T&T Clark, 2008), 189, "the New Testament texts do not offer enough information to reconstruct a uniform 'early Christian view' of the physical universe. . . . There is no chapter and verse citation which demands to be read against Galileo or Copernicus."

for instance, God actually killed dragons when creating the world—that way lies the polytheistic myths of Israel's pagan neighbors. Scripture's cosmological symbolism belongs to its religious description of the world as a complex, ordered reality where God is active and humans are touched by forces they cannot always see, prompting them to cast themselves fearfully upon God, cultivating wisdom, humility, and wonder. The symbolic cosmological language of Scripture may often strike us as strange and alien, but in this regard it draws us out of our typically dull ways of thinking about God, the world, and ourselves.

Poetry Both Conceals and Reveals

Poetic images and symbols also describe creation's order in ways that both conceal and reveal. This too illustrates how poetry is the proper language of creation, for two reasons. First, Scripture's poetic forms voice an awareness of creation's meaning as a gift of the Creator's wisdom, power, and righteousness. That meaning, therefore, is always more than we can quite capture. In Ecclesiastes, Qoheleth contrasts the reliably cyclical order of creation with the inconstancy of human life.

> A generation goes, and a generation comes,
>   but the earth remains forever. (Eccl. 1:4)

Day by day, the sun, wind, and waters all move unceasingly within the boundaries the Creator gives them, but the boundaries of human life are written in the dirt. Whatever learning or wisdom someone achieves, it's nothing genuinely "new" for those who live "under the sun" (Eccl. 1:9). This leads Qoheleth to the insight that

> all words are full of weariness;
>   a man cannot utter it;

> the eye is not satisfied with seeing,
> nor the ear filled with hearing. (Eccl. 1:8)[38]

He sees creation, yet he does not see. And this experience frustrates.

Creation's good order and boundaries contrast with the transience of our personal lives. We yearn to speak, see, and hear more than any boundary allows, but no one can exhaustively speak, see, hear, or remember the things of creation and life "under the sun." Life is not wearisome, but our inability to grasp and understand everything can leave us restless unless we make peace with our limits. Job learns this when God patiently questions him about creation, beginning with whether Job knows about the boundaries of the earth and sea (Job 38:4–11). As we will see in later chapters, regardless of our scientific or historical knowledge, we cannot plumb the depths of creation's secrets. The deepest truths about creation and its order come to us in poetic language because poetry preserves their mystery and discourages idle curiosity.

Second, then, just like poetry, creation's order requires careful, loving attention because it does not interpret itself. This means that to learn wisdom, we will have to be studious, attentive to God's book of nature, always mindful that its interpretation is subordinate to the book of Scripture. Nevertheless, we must read both books. Part of the difficulty with science-and-religion debates is that they typically refuse to let these two books speak in their own languages.[39] Hence, on all sides of these debates, one readily finds treatments of the Bible as if it were a science book or trying haphazardly to be one. However, Scripture speaks

38. It is not "all things" that are full of weariness (as the ESV has it) but "all words." See Christopher R. Seitz, *The Elder Testament: Canon, Theology, Trinity* (Baylor, 2018), 234–36.

39. Radner, *A Time to Keep*, 246–47.

poetically and doxologically about creation because even as it conceals some of creation's mysteries, what it reveals concerns creation's meaning and order in relation to God. When we try, as we should, to understand how Scripture's teaching relates to contemporary science or the latest archaeological findings from the Ancient Near East, we must avoid "the twin excesses" of veneration and condemnation.[40] That is, we must refuse the unbelieving temptation that these sources can either vindicate or invalidate God's written word, which is self-authenticating. The doctrine of creation concerns the truth about created reality, which is much broader and deeper than the universe's natural history. Love for this truth must be "patient" (1 Cor. 13:4). Accepting this fact makes us *slow* on the uptake, giving time and space for the joyful work of interpretation, repentant attention to the words of life.[41] We may therefore listen patiently to other sciences, confident that whatever is ultimately true in them will cohere with the correct interpretation of Holy Scripture.

Conclusion

The opening lines of Genesis are unequivocal: "In the beginning." Not *a* beginning, but *the* beginning of all things, the reader included. It summons us to contemplate our past and therefore all the present circumstances of our lives and hopes for the future, all that we see around us in the world and that everyone experiences, in light of what has come before us and none have experienced. Genesis begins as an act of tutored remembrance. We are not our own, but we belong to God and must tune our lives to God's will.

40. Blocher, *In the Beginning*, 24. Somewhat similarly, Johann Auer, *Die Welt, Gottes Schöpfung* (Pustet, 1975), 24, is correct when he observes that for much of its modern history, the doctrine of creation has been distorted by excessive attention to philosophical apologetics and the concern "to understand and parrot the scientific knowledge of the world."

41. Jean-Yves Lacoste, "More Haste, Less Speed in Theology," trans. Oliver O'Donovan, *International Journal of Systematic Theology* 9, no. 3 (2007): 263–82.

Creation's doxological character is taught to us in the hexaemeron and its echoes throughout Scripture. We have seen this in how the hexaemeron functions like a hymn, like a liturgy, and why it speaks to us with poetry and symbolism. There is a valuable hermeneutical lesson in all this: The form in which Scripture teaches us about creation is part of the doctrine's content. We will see later how creatures are whole things, unities of their form and their content. One thing a biblical understanding of creation must affirm is the unity of form and content, even within Scripture. Scripture speaks about creation in doxological tones, liturgical forms, and poetic symbols because creation is ordered to the praise of God, to be used for the praise of God, and points beyond itself to God.

Debates continue about how best to read the hexaemeron, and this too is "nothing new under the sun." According to Augustine's famous advice for reading Scripture, good readings foster the love of God and love of neighbor.[42] At minimum, poor readings do not tell us how we should order our time and steward the fruits of our labors. The reading in this chapter lays bare some of the claims the doctrine of creation makes upon our lives, possessions, and loves—though what that looks like awaits further development beyond this chapter. This does not make our interpretation inerrant. It will not settle debates about how to read this text, nor need it. All it does is provide us with a pilgrim's grip on the text: one that is traveling a path, going somewhere, but has not yet arrived. Such is the nature of theology! Our first concern is for the truth of Scripture, for which reason we must remain open to better readings, "not insisting on this one in such a way as to contend that nothing else preferable can be found."[43]

---

42. Augustine, *Teaching Christianity* 1.35.39–1.40.44 (*WSA* I/11:123–26).

43. Augustine, *Literal Meaning of Genesis* 4.28.45 (trans. Edmund Hill, *WSA* I/13:268).

2

God's Musicality

The Trinity and Creation

As we listen to the Creator's hymn, we are drawn into the doxology of creation—a song meant to elicit singing. One of the first things theology must explore is how this song relates to the divine singer. To be a creature is to be part of what happens "when God's musicality opens" outwardly, so we must consider the background to creation's music in the musical life of the Holy Trinity.[1] Before speaking of creatures, we must speak of the Creator. After all, the hymn would say nothing about creatures unless it were talking about the works *of the Creator*. There is an intrinsic order that theological thinking must observe if our thoughts are subject to Scripture: first God, then God's works. This order tells us something important.

1. Robert W. Jenson, *Systematic Theology*, vol. 2, *The Works of God* (Oxford University Press, 2001), 39. However, there are significant differences between my approach to God's "musicality" and Jenson's.

Every mistaken belief about creation masks a larger mistaken belief about God.[2] If we believe creatures are worthless, it's because we believe God withholds worth from creatures. If we think creatures are really just parts of God, it's because we believe God doesn't create so much as expand or mutate. If we deny any meaningful agency and freedom to creatures, it's because we think God is the only real agent. These sorts of errors suspect that God can't or won't give creatures their own reality, worth, and agency because God is either limited in his creative power or miserly. Clarity about God's creation follows from clarity about who the Creator is.

What, then, should we confess about the Creator? The ultimate answer would be an entire doctrine of God, exploring his divine perfections and the distinct persons of the Trinity. Our focus is narrower. This chapter begins with some direct reflections on God's readiness, freedom, and generosity as the Creator. Considering these points will lay the foundation for the following chapters to explore God's creative act and its effects in greater detail. We will pattern our reflections after the hymn of the heavenly creatures around God's throne in heaven:

> Worthy are you, our Lord and God,
>   to receive glory and honor and power,
> for you created all things,
>   and by your will they existed and were created.
>   (Rev. 4:11)

Each section of this chapter will return to this text and unfold as an observation on it.

2. Aquinas, *Summa contra Gentiles* II, c. 3. Unless otherwise stated, references to Aquinas's works are from the editions available on the Aquinas Institute's website: https://aquinas.cc/la/en/~ST.I , accessed August 2024.

The Trinity's Musicality: God's Readiness to Create

The first thing to consider is why the heavenly creatures confess the Creator as "worthy" to be praised for having created. In part, this means that creation is a praiseworthy act of God. And here we discover a simple yet profound truth. Creation is a praiseworthy act because it fits with who God is; it rhymes with his own "musicality." By creating, God does not contradict himself but expresses the fullness and fruitfulness of his own goodness. Because God is fruitful in himself, he is ready to make other things fruitful as their Creator. All this is another way of saying that God can sing because God is eternally musical. This is the thought we must explore in this section. The doctrine of God gives us the only sure footing for the doctrine of creation. Indeed, the theme of God's musicality helps us understand how creation is more like a song than a sculpture, which is carved from something else, or a still-life painting, in which all movement is frozen.

With the idea of God's "musicality," we are concerned with God's life of fruitful love, revealed to us in the Trinity. Understanding God's triune life as a fruitful life of love will help us see how the song of creation "rhymes" with God's musicality in at least two ways. First, God's musicality shows how creation bears some similarity to who God is (something we will especially explore in later chapters). Second, and more to our present purposes, God's musicality proves that God is always already prepared to create. If you know God's character, then creation isn't the sort of thing you'd be surprised to see God do. We'll consider, first, God's goodness and then the infinite communication of that goodness in the Trinity's life of fruitful love.

God's Goodness

In order to understand God's life of fruitful love, we must first understand the background of God's love in his goodness. For, as we will see, love is a way of communicating goodness to another. Scripture testifies to God's goodness constantly, describing him not only as intrinsically good but also as the source and goal of all good things. "Good and upright is the LORD" (Ps. 25:8); "Oh, taste and see that the LORD is good!" (Ps. 34:8). When we look at these and similar statements about God's goodness across Scripture, we discover that God's goodness is not only food for thought but especially food for our affections. Because God is good, we are drawn to him with everything we are. God's goodness means that he is both desirable and inclined to communicate his goodness, to share it.[3]

First, as the highest good and source of all good things (James 1:17), God's uncreated goodness is *desirable* above all other goods. Like a deer panting for water, the psalmist says,

> My soul thirsts for God,
> for the living God. (Ps. 42:2)

David knows that if he drinks from this fountain, his thirst will be quenched, because "those who seek the LORD lack no good thing" (Ps. 34:10). "The LORD is good to all," David confesses elsewhere, for God satisfies "the desire of every living thing" (Ps. 145:9, 16). All our desires, especially for mundane goods, fade in comparison with desire for God's goodness.

> Whom have I in heaven but you?
> And there is nothing on earth that I desire besides you.
> (Ps. 73:25; cf. Matt. 19:17)

Second, because God's goodness is desirable above all things, God is also greatly inclined to communicate it. That is to say, the desirability and *communicativeness* of God's good-

3. Aquinas, *Summa theologiae* I, qq. 5–6.

ness go together. Everyday experience echoes this truth faintly. Whenever we find something "good" in this world, we delight in sharing it with others. We often spread the word about a favorite recipe, book, hiking trail, fishing hole, or film because goodness loves company far more than misery. It's almost irresistible to keep these experiences to ourselves. The good we enjoy pulls us out of ourselves and diffuses itself to others. This truth about goodness tells us something profound, since every good we can desire comes from God, who created it by "communicating" some likeness of his own goodness to it. But what does it tell us about God's goodness in himself?

Most of all, we need to be clear about what our experience of goodness as desirable and communicative does *not* tell us about God's goodness. For instance, although God's goodness is desirable *to us*, this doesn't therefore mean that it is desirable *to God*. If we carefully examine our language, we find that it would not be proper to say that God "desires" his own goodness (or any other good), insofar as desire is always for something absent. But no good is absent from God, for he is the source of all good things and is himself his own goodness. Desire in this sense doesn't have any place in God.[4] If God doesn't desire his own goodness, then the only thing left for him is to love and enjoy it. Whereas desire strives to possess some good, love and enjoyment crown our chaste possession of goods. God's pure love of his own goodness has infinitely more than "desire" because he eternally possesses what every desire ultimately seeks.

Once we understand this, then we can see what our experience of goodness as desirable and communicative tells us about

4. Augustine, *Expositions of the Psalms* 118.8.4 (trans. Maria Boulding, *WSA* III/19:375–76). If we nevertheless speak of God desiring things, it is not in the sense that he lacks some good without which he is incomplete; it typically means that God wills and pursues something, that it pleases him (cf. Pss. 68:16; 132:13–14).

God's own goodness: Because God's goodness is intrinsically delightful, it delights God to communicate it. This is the transcendent foundation for why good things draw forth desire and prompt their communication to others. God's goodness does this, so all reflections of it do as well. The psalmist thus confesses of God, "You are good and do good" (Ps. 119:68). God's being good and doing good are here inseparable from one another, for he is both desirable and communicative in the same breath. Hence, God's goodness is his perfection "through which he can communicate himself and deserves to be desired, and must be."[5]

The Trinity's Fruitful Life of Love

God is good and does good because God is desirable above all things and intrinsically communicative. God has a sort of natural inclination to share himself. Since there is no higher good than God's own goodness, he is naturally and necessarily inclined toward his own goodness. This is the basis for everything he does. This inclination is his "most wise propensity toward himself as the highest end, and toward the creatures, on account of himself, as the means."[6] Here is the key to God's musicality: God's life is a life of love, and he loves all others things in order to share that love with them. To speak of God's "propensity" is therefore to speak of his love's tendency or inclination to share his goodness. This is the root, as it were, of his musicality.

Now, God's propensity to share his goodness, his love, looks different in God than it does in the world. Within the world, God's propensity to share his goodness is an act of freedom, the sort of freedom that can only come with love that is chaste

5. Petrus van Mastricht, *Theoretical-Practical Theology*, trans. Todd M. Rester, ed. Joel R. Beeke, vol. 2, *Faith in the Triune God* (Reformation Heritage, 2019), 1.2.16.vii (331).

6. Van Mastricht, *Theoretical-Practical Theology* 1.2.15.viii (2:297).

or pure. God is not simply bubbling over with goodness, unable to avoid spilling everywhere indiscriminately. He is not unchaste or promiscuous. As the "blessed and only sovereign," God is Lord over the communication of his goodness to others (1 Tim. 6:15). Ultimately, this is because God has no needs or desires that could conflict with loving others without ulterior motives. He loves his own goodness and has everything that could be wanted. God's love is therefore pure, wholehearted love. His propensity to share his goodness is the propensity of chaste love: to love others "non-possessively," without damage to their freedom and dignity.[7] Therefore, as God turns the propensity of his goodness toward the world, he acts for love of his own goodness: to communicate it, not to achieve something he doesn't have.[8]

Theology speaks of God's propensity to share himself within the world by many names, following his revelation of himself to Moses on Mount Sinai:

> The Lord, the Lord, a God merciful and gracious, slow to anger, and abounding in steadfast love and faithfulness, keeping steadfast love for thousands, forgiving iniquity and transgression and sin, but who will by no means clear the guilty, visiting the iniquity of the fathers on the children and the children's children, to the third and fourth generation. (Ex. 34:6–7; cf. 33:19)

God's propensity to love others—willing them good and doing good to them—therefore can be seen in his mercy, grace, and patience.[9]

---

7. See Erik Varden, *Chastity: Reconciliation of the Senses* (Bloomsbury, 2023), 102–12.
8. Aquinas, *De potentia* q. 3, a. 15, ad 14.
9. Willing good to others is God's *benevolence*, and doing good to them is his *beneficence*.

However, God's propensity to share himself within himself looks different from all this. Within God, there is no misery that needs mercy, no disfavor that requires grace, no aversion that requires patience, but there is loving fellowship and mutual delight between Father, Son, and Holy Spirit.[10] "God is love" (1 John 4:8). But not just any kind of love. God's love within his own life is *fruitful* love. The propensity of God to share himself in pure love is manifest in his eternal life of fruitfulness.[11] Here is the summit of his musicality.

God's fruitful life of love consists in the natural, necessary communication of God's goodness—its entire, infinite excellence—from the Father to the Son and the Spirit. The Trinity's eternal relations show that God's life is not barren, like a dead tree or a dry fount. Rather, God's eternal life has a "natural fecundity," or fruitfulness, in which the Father begets and breathes two divine persons who share his same nature.[12] Cyril of Alexandria thus likens the Son to the fruit of the Father's essence, and the Spirit to the living fragrance of that same essence, which makes the fruit known.[13] As the Son glorifies the Father and makes him known to us, "the tree is known by its fruit" (Matt. 12:33).[14] The propensity of God's goodness, his pure love, is eternally fruitful in the divine processions of the Son and the Spirit from the Father. When God reveals these truths to us, "the wealth of the divine goodness comes into prominence. . . . Here we perceive that He is good not only because He possesses infinite goods, but that He is good, infinitely good, in the complete communication of His goods."[15]

10. Van Mastricht, *Theoretical-Practical Theology* 1.2.17.viii (2:351).

11. Leonardus Lessius, *De perfectionibus moribusque divinis* (Paris, 1620), 9.1.2 (106).

12. John of Damascus, *Exact Exposition of the Orthodox Faith* 8 (PPS 62:72).

13. Cyril of Alexandria, *Commentary on John* 11.1–2, trans. David R. Maxwell, ed. Joel C. Elowsky, Ancient Christian Texts (IVP Academic, 2013), 2:258–60.

14. Cyril of Alexandria, *Commentary on John* 11.6 (2:277).

15. Matthias Joseph Scheeben, *The Mysteries of Christianity*, trans. Cyril Vollert (Herder & Herder, 1946), 128. This does not mean that we could "prove" the doctrine

The Trinity's fruitful life of love reveals to us the infinite depths of God's propensity to share himself, his musicality. Because of this propensity of love, God is eternally disposed to communicate himself *also* in a finite manner to others, to establish fellowship with creatures and crown it with delight. On account of his goodness, then, God is eternally ready to create. Because God is fruitful in himself, he loves to cultivate fruitfulness in his creation. The song of creation thus "rhymes" with God's intrinsic musicality. This is what it means to say that creation is "worthy" of God. Creation is consistent with God's life of fruitful love. We will therefore be able to be perceive creation aright when we encounter it as a sign of God's fruitful love meant to imitate, in its own ways, his fruitfulness.

The Opening of God's Musicality: God's Creative Freedom

God is good and naturally communicates his goodness within himself in the blossoming love of the Father, Son, and Holy Spirit. Because God's love is fruitful in himself, he is ready to create echoes of this fruitfulness in others. God's musicality is ready to open outwardly, to unfold into song. However, this insight raises the question of whether creation is something God is compelled to do. If God naturally communicates his goodness, then would he not necessarily seek to communicate himself to as many things as possible? Does this not make creation an inevitability? On the contrary, in the text we considered above, the angelic creatures praise God for creating by his "will" (Rev. 4:11). Creation is therefore an act of God's

---

of the Trinity from the mere concept of goodness's communicative nature. See here Bonaventure, *Itinerarium mentis in Deum* 6.1–3; Aquinas, *Summa theologiae* I, q. 32, a. 1, ad 2.

freedom, not something imposed upon him. We may appreciate this if we consider (1) the distinction between God's internal and external works and (2) how God creates freely.

God's Internal and External Works

The distinction we considered above, between God's love within the world and within himself, rests upon an important distinction between God's internal and external works. Although the language of "internal" and "external" is spatial, the distinction is not between space "within" God and "outside" him, as if God were a measurable three-dimensional object. The distinction is instead about an activity that belongs to the fullness of God's uncreated life versus one that belongs to God's plan to make and fulfill created life. At its most basic, then, God's internal works are those "in which nothing is produced outside of God or different from God," whereas the external works produce something "different from God."[16] Internal acts arise within God and stay there because they are directed to himself. Something like this happens when we understand some truth, since our act of understanding *on its own* doesn't affect or change anything outside us. External works, on the contrary, arise within God but don't remain there; they eventually pour forth onto something else. This is similar to how we make plans and then carry them out.

Distinguishing between God's internal and external works helps us recognize how some of them are necessary and some contingent. We may think of this like a cascading fountain, beginning with God's internal activity, flowing down to his internal works, and eventually to God's external works.

16. Petrus van Mastricht, *Theoretical-Practical Theology*, trans. Todd M. Rester, ed. Joel R. Beeke, vol. 3, *The Works of God and the Fall of Man* (Reformation Heritage, 2019), 1.3.1.vii (5).

God's *internal activity* is the same as his musicality. These are acts without which God would not be God, such as the Father's eternal begetting of the Son and the eternal breathing of the Spirit from both Father and Son. This internal activity is necessary because it describes God's own eternal life of fruitful love, without which there would be no created life. God's *internal works* differ from his internal activity because they are not necessary, but contingent. These internal works include God's plan or decree to create and redeem creatures for his glory (Isa. 46:9–10; Acts 4:28; Eph. 1:11). Like all plans, God's plans depend on his will and counsel. Here is where we locate the beginning of God opening his musicality outwardly.

God's *external works* overflow from these contingent internal works the way executing a plan follows planning itself. Creation is the first of these outer works. Because God has decreed before the foundations of the world that he would create and redeem a people for himself, he executes this plan by creating those foundations and those people. These distinctions help us to understand how creation is free and therefore a gift of God's love.

God's Freedom to Create

God's freedom in creation begins with its contingency. Although God's musicality means he is ready to create, he does not thereby need to create. God's love is his propensity to communicate his goodness. Yet this propensity within God needs no outlet to find satisfaction, because that tendency eternally rests in the Father's full communication of his goodness to the Son and the Spirit. This is the only necessary communication that follows from God's propensity to communicate his goodness. If God turns this propensity toward something else, it is not because he cannot help himself or ought to meet some demand. It can only be because he loves to do this, he delights in doing it. Because God's propensity rests in his own goodness, he is not miserly "but rather wishes everyone to exist, in order to exercise his kindness."[17] God's fruitful goodness means that he loves to create, not that he must. Creation is therefore a work of free love, being neither necessary nor arbitrary.

First, *creation is not necessary*. God "works all things according to the counsel *of his will*" (Eph. 1:11). God's external works flow from *free* counsel, not mere counsel. That is to say, creation is not the necessary consequence of God knowing his own goodness and its worthiness to be shared by others. God's propensity to communicate himself is not a compulsion. Otherwise, creation would be necessary for God to be God.[18] If that were the case, then creation would be something God owed to himself. And from here, it's a small step to God owing it to his own goodness to give creatures every good. Such a misconception is popular in some contemporary theologies that promote universalism.

These mistaken views overlook God's lordship. God did not need to create, nor was he compelled to do so by any lack or obligation from within or without. "The God who made the world and everything in it, being Lord of heaven and earth, does not live in temples made by man, nor is he served by human hands, as though he needed anything, since he himself gives to all mankind life and breath and everything" (Acts 17:24–25; cf. Ps. 50:7–15). Creation is not the satisfaction of some obligation, but a gift. It is the first of the good gifts that come from the Father of lights (James 1:17–18).

---

17. Athanasius, *Contra Gentes* 41, in *Contra Gentes and De Incarnatione*, ed. and trans. Robert W. Thomson (Oxford University Press, 1971), 115.

18. See Aquinas, *Summa theologiae* I, q. 65, a. 2, ad 3; *Commentary on the Psalms* 24.218.

Second, *creation is not arbitrary*. God "works all things according to the *counsel* of his will" (Eph. 1:11). God's external works are not mere products of impulsive will, but they rest upon the deepest counsel. God did not create "just because," on a whim. If he did, creation would be the result of a sudden urge. And whenever we act on sudden urges, wisdom is typically not in the picture. An arbitrary creation would be a hot mess, perhaps even meaningless. Folks who feel that it is might resonate with the irreverent line from the beginning of Douglas Adams's book *The Restaurant at the End of the Universe*: "The story so far: In the beginning the Universe was created. This has made a lot of people very angry and been widely regarded as a bad move."[19] Such a "creation" would be noise rather than music, an act of neglect rather than provision. On the contrary, creation is an act of God's unsearchable wisdom.

> In wisdom you have made them all;
> the earth is full of your creatures. (Ps. 104:24)

Creating by his wisdom (Prov. 3:19), God gives things the deepest meaning, one echoing his own eternal life as he illustrates within us his own glory, "that which shines forth in God's goodness."[20]

God opens his musicality outwardly with freedom and wisdom because his fruitful love is chaste and pure. Unfolding his musical life toward us, he loves us in a way that gives without need of return. And he guides all things with the deepest wisdom and meaning; for, as we must now consider, he guides them to his glory.

---

19. Douglas Adams, *The Restaurant at the End of the Universe*, The Hitchhiker's Guide to the Galaxy 2 (1980; repr., Del Rey, 1995), 1.

20. John Calvin, *Commentary on Ephesians* 1:12 (CO 51:152).

Why God Opens His Musicality: Creation's Purposes and End

Our final consideration in this chapter concerns *why* God opens his musicality toward creatures. As we saw earlier, the creatures around God's throne confess,

> You created all things,
> and by your will they existed and were created.
> (Rev. 4:11)

This last phrase, "existed and were created," is strange because it mentions the existence of things before their creation. However we interpret this, it suggests that there is an order and purpose to God's creative activity.[21] Crowning our consideration of God's readiness and freedom as the Creator is the wisdom and purpose with which he orders all things. What is creation for, and how does it relate to the other ways God communicates his goodness, such as in redemption (grace) and in consummation (glory)? Is creation just an unrefined stage for redemption, or does it have some significance of its own? Why does God sing this song and not just skip straight to the "new song"? To answer these questions, we must consider the "end" of creation, that for which it is made, the fulfillment of its purpose.

An end is much broader and more significant than an "ending," a mere conclusion. Ends describe a thing's state of flourishing, both the goal toward which something naturally moves when it's unhindered and the full maturity and wholeness in which it flourishes as God intends. So, for example, the end of an acorn is to germinate in the earth and grow into a full

21. This point holds for several different interpretations of this phrase. Among others, see G. K. Beale, *The Book of Revelation: A Commentary on the Greek Text*, New International Greek Testament Commentary (Eerdmans, 1999), 335–36; Henry Barclay Swete, *The Apocalypse of St. John: The Greek Text with Introduction, Notes, and Indices* (Macmillan, 1906), 74.

oak tree. And the end of an oak tree is to flourish as an oak tree, produce acorns, provide shade, shelter squirrels, and so forth. Now, as soon as we recognize that things have ends, we must distinguish ends from purposes.[22] The purposes of a real estate developer might involve chopping down the oak tree to make room for a driveway, which is not the oak tree's state of unhindered flourishing. However, purposes can also align with ends. I might plant an oak tree precisely because I want some shade in my yard, a place for birds and squirrels to congregate, and so forth. In this case, my purposes with the oak tree coincide with its own flourishing. All the same, it's serious business distinguishing ends and purposes. Is a lawyer trustworthy if he confuses his own purposes of making money and a name for himself with the ends of the law itself? With that in mind, we may see how every individual creature has an end, as does the creation collectively. There are two ways to consider creation's end or goal: intrinsically or extrinsically.

In one way, creation achieves its intrinsic goal by simply flourishing as the good reality God made. God intends creatures to flourish in ways befitting their natures, in relation both to themselves and to others. This flourishing begins in relation to their own habitats and the creatures immediately surrounding them, extending to the many ecological spheres that intersect within them, and finally in their subordination to humans, made in God's image.[23] These relations contribute to creation's grand "harmony." For example, in themselves, bees achieve their end by flourishing as bees, doing what bees are supposed to do, playing their role in the cosmic tapestry of living things.

---

22. Francis Slade, "On the Ontological Priority of Ends and Its Relevance to the Narrative Arts," in *Beauty, Art, and the Polis*, ed. Alice Ramos (Catholic University of America Press, 2000), 58–69.

23. Aquinas, *Summa theologiae* I, q. 65, a. 2. In other words, creation's intrinsic end can be considered with regard to its parts' relations to their works, those parts' relations to one another, and their relations to the whole.

In relation to other creatures, bees achieve their end along much the same lines: pollinating plants and trees, serving the biodiversity of their environments, the health of soils, and more. In relation to the whole, the loss of bees would be significant for life as we know it. In relation to humans, then, bees benefit us not only by sustaining the ecosystem but also by giving us honey, wax, and venom for all manner of purposes. Thus, we may appreciate how creation has its own intrinsic ends and purposiveness. God loves life and its fruitfulness because God's life is fruitful love.

Yet life is not merely about living. Creation also has an extrinsic end in terms of the whole's relation to God. All creatures are ordered to God as their extrinsic or ultimate end, "in so far as the divine goodness is reflected through them and thus his glory manifested."[24] We may understand this by reflecting for a moment on why we do the things we do. As we saw earlier, whenever we seek after something, we do so because we find it good or desirable. This remains true even though some desirable things—like our neighbor's goods—are illicit for us (Ex. 20:17). Whatever we desire is good in some sense; otherwise we would not desire it. But our desires themselves can be very evil.

> The heart is deceitful above all things,
>   and desperately sick. (Jer. 17:9)

Sin makes it possible for us to twist something's goodness toward purposes completely at odds with its end, which can result in extreme horrors. God's purity is his freedom from these dynamics of desire and therefore covetousness. There is no good-

24. Aquinas, *Summa theologiae* I, q. 65, a. 2. When quoted, translations are from the Blackfriars edition of the *Summa Theologiae*, 61 vols. (McGraw-Hill, 1964–1980; Cambridge University Press, 2006). Scripture teaches this explicitly: "Bring my sons from afar / and my daughters from the ends of the earth, / everyone who is called by my name, / whom I created for my glory" (Isa. 43:6–7; cf. 48:11).

ness higher than God's own. Nothing can bring him greater enjoyment than he has in himself. And insofar as every act aims at some end, God's acts cannot reach higher than himself. God is his own "end," as it were. God therefore "acts because of his goodness not as though he desires something he does not have, but because he desires to communicate what he does have: for he acts not from desire, but from love of the end."[25]

God's acts spring from God's delight in his own goodness, and they are meant to draw others into that delight. God therefore creates by ordering all things to his own goodness, which is the only way God acts. All creatures have God's goodness as their end, so that they might reflect it and taste it in some way. This is how things "glorify" God—by receiving and manifesting his goodness in their own ways. Naturally, not all creatures do this in the same way (Pss. 19, 148). Irrational creatures—animals and inanimate things—have God as their end in the sense that they yearn for and receive God's goodness in the ways they can (Ps. 145:15–16).[26] Rational creatures—angels and humans—have God as their end in a special way, since they can taste and see that God is good spiritually, through knowing and loving God (Ps. 34:8). Bees cannot do this; they lack the powers for it. Not only do humans have powers to receive God's goodness and glorify him more than irrational creatures, but by grace we may "be made glorious in the glory of God" and "perceive all good as both from His glory and to His glory" (see John 17:22; Rom. 8:30).[27]

25. Aquinas, *De potentia* q. 3, a. 15, ad 14, in *St. Thomas Aquinas: On Creation (Quaestiones Disputatae de Potentia Dei, Q. 3)*, trans. S. C. Selner-Wright (Catholic University of America Press, 2011).

26. Aquinas, *Commentary on the Sentences*, bk. 2, d. 1, q. 2, a. 2, ad 4.

27. Franciscus Junius, *A Treatise on True Theology*, trans. David Noe (Reformation Heritage, 2014), thesis 33 (211); cf. also Junius, *Theses theologicae* 16.3, in *Opuscula theologica selecta*, ed. Abraham Kuyper (Amsterdam, 1882), 155; Van Mastricht, *Theoretical-Practical Theology* 1.3.5.xviii (3:113); Christoph Schwöbel, "God, Creation and the Christian Community," in *The Doctrine of Creation: Essays in Dogmatics, History and Philosophy*, ed. Colin E. Gunton (T&T Clark, 2004), 149–76.

Such distinctions between creation's intrinsic ends and its ultimate end help us understand how creation is related to eschatology, how the original song relates to the "new song." On the one hand, all God's works are ordered to his glory as their ultimate end. God's glory is the end of predestining people for adoption (Eph. 1:5–6), giving them an inheritance and a new life (Eph. 1:11–12), and finally making them his own possession (Eph. 1:14).[28] Hence, "all things" are "from him and through him and to him. . . . To him be glory forever" (Rom. 11:36). Everything is related to God's glory as its ultimate end, in this sense. Yet everything still has its own role in the grand scheme. To borrow an image from Scripture, all God's works are like a ladder that takes us to God himself. In this image, the side rails of the ladder represent God's wisdom and decree because they stretch from the ground and pierce the heavens, holding together all the rungs. The lowest rungs comprise God's works of "nature," such as creation and providence. We can lean on these without leaving the ground. The next highest rungs include God's works of "grace," which embrace what he does to reconcile and heal lost sinners. These rungs take us from the ground and lead us ever higher. Yet the topmost rungs disappear from sight, clouded with the future. These are God's works of "glory," embracing the last things: Christ's return, the judgment, and the new creation. At the very top of the ladder is the destination: God himself in his glory. We cannot reach the higher rungs without the lower ones, but the higher we climb, the clearer our view of the destination becomes. The ladder leads to one destination alone. Nevertheless, each distinct rung is still necessary in its own way, having its own integrity and purpose.

28. Calvin, *Commentary on Ephesians* 1:14, comments: "We should not treat the oft-repeated commemoration of God's glory as something superfluous, for nothing can be said in excess of an infinite reality. . . . For this theme is such that if both angels and men were to unfold their whole eloquence, they would still fall short of its greatness" (*CO* 51:154).

Somewhat similar to this ladder imagery, God's end for every one of his works is his own glory, but those works have distinct motives or purposes. Thus, God's end for creation is his own glory, but his purpose for creation is that it achieves its intrinsic, natural end: "namely, that all things should exist agreeably according to nature."[29] Likewise, God's end for the incarnation of his Son is his glory, whereas its purpose is "to save sinners" (1 Tim. 1:15; cf. Luke 19:10) and "to destroy the works of the devil" (1 John 3:8). The purposes of God's works of nature and grace are distinct, whereas their end is identical. And in the grand design of God, these purposes are inseparable from one another because the creation God intends is one that will need to be saved from the grip of sin and death (Rom. 8:19–22).[30] Creation is therefore inseparable from redemption and glorification but nevertheless distinct and should not be confused with them.[31]

Before concluding, we must be careful not to misunderstand what it means for God to create everything for his glory. Critics object that this idea makes God rather self-preoccupied or ultimately in need of creatures to reassure him of his divinity. Such concerns are ultimately misplaced. When God seeks his own glory, this does not mean that he diminishes the dignity of human beings by treating them as a mere means, nor that his love is selfish or vain. Someone is vainglorious when he or she

29. Junius, *Theses theologicae* 15.4 (152).

30. This raises the question of whether the Son would have become incarnate apart from sin. We do not have space to address the issue sufficiently here. Aquinas opined that the "question is not one of great importance," because it concerns a hypothetical situation that God did not will (Aquinas, *Commentary on 1 Timothy* 1.4.40). My argument is largely in agreement: Christ *could* have become incarnate apart from sin if God so willed, but Scripture nowhere suggests unambiguously that Christ *would* have.

31. This is relevant for art. Not everything valuable concerns redemption or its secularized counterfeits. Truth, goodness, and beauty may be discovered in creation. Where this lesson is ignored, so-called art becomes very preachy and sentimental in order to mask the absence of hard-won insights into reality—insights that are acquired through experience and contemplation, not infused by grace.

pursues glory for the wrong reasons, from the wrong people, or with the wrong motives.[32] None of these apply to God. His glory does not come at the expense of others. It is right for God to pursue his glory, since his supreme goodness not only is worthy of all honor and glory (Rev. 4:11) but also satisfies those who taste and see it (Pss. 27:4; 34:8; 103:5). There is no greater good than God's, and so no greater end (Ps. 16:2; Mark 10:18). If God directed all things to something short of himself, he would want lesser goods for them. God makes himself glorious among us for our sake, not for his, so that we may share in the knowledge of his praiseworthiness and delight in him as he delights in himself. God's love dignifies us by opening our eyes to discover in him the source of all honor and dignity. God's glory works to our benefit.[33]

It is therefore good news for creatures that God's glory is the goal of God's works. Doxologies like Paul's "to him be glory forever" (Rom. 11:36)[34] are responses to God showing his glory, making his goodness and beauty unmistakably known in some way (Ps. 145:7). Angels respond this way to God in heaven (Ps. 29:9). Wayfaring humans respond similarly on earth (Heb. 13:21). When God's people get a glimpse of his glory, they rejoice in fruitfulness and are filled with peace.

> The wilderness and the dry land shall be glad;
>   the desert shall rejoice and blossom like the crocus;
> it shall blossom abundantly
>   and rejoice with joy and singing. . . .
> They shall see the glory of the Lord. (Isa. 35:1–2;
>   cf. 40:1–5)

32. Aquinas, *Summa theologiae* II-II, q. 132, a. 1.
33. Junius, *Theses theologicae* 14.2 (149).
34. Cf. Rom. 16:27; Eph. 3:21; Phil. 4:20; 1 Tim. 1:17; Heb. 13:21; 1 Pet. 4:11; 2 Pet. 3:18; Jude 25; Rev. 1:6; 4:11; 5:11–13.

Hence, the angels sing,

> Glory to God in the highest,
> and on earth peace among those with whom he is
> pleased! (Luke 2:14; cf. Isa. 9:6)

God opens his own musicality to open our lips, to make us fully resonant with song.

Conclusion

The angelic praise of the Creator as "worthy" to receive glory, honor, and power carries wide-ranging significance.[35] At its core, it voices that there is a "fit" between who the Creator is and his creative activity. Ultimately, this fit is revealed in the musicality of God's life as Father, Son, and Holy Spirit. This is one reason why knowledge of the Trinity is "necessary . . . in order to have a right view of the creation of things."[36] Because God's triune musicality is infinitely communicative and fruitful, God can also communicate goods to us without adding to or diminishing his goodness. Without creatures, God would be just as good, loving, and fruitful as he is with creatures. God does not become musical when he sings the song of creation, but he displays his own musicality toward others. God communicates himself to summon communicants; he glorifies himself to glorify others; he sings to evoke song. It remains for us to consider in the following chapters the "singing" itself, the act of creating, as well as the "song," the creation itself.

35. For further reflections on its implications for biblical exegesis, see R. B. Jamieson and Tyler Wittman, *Biblical Reasoning: Christological and Trinitarian Rules for Exegesis* (Baker Academic, 2022), 63–90.

36. Aquinas, *Summa theologiae* I, q. 32, a. 1, ad 3.

3

How God Sings

Creation Out of Nothing and the Creator's Generosity

Opening his own musicality toward another, God orchestrates the creation song via his own singing. Yet the song doesn't begin like other songs. Nor is the singing something we can imagine. It's all very different because God isn't an ordinary singer. Unless we grasp this, we will fatally misunderstand the character of the Creator's song.

Ordinarily, songs arise "out of" many things, such as instruments, influences, cultural moments, experiences, ambitions, and more. Artists influence other artists, and songs often emerge from a host of muses. None of this is true of God. There are no instruments for him to employ, no influences acting upon him, no experiences he feels compelled to express in music, no thirst for greatness he must quench. He is not inspired by any ideals transcending him. Seeking to understand this song, we can look no further than God. It is "from" God alone (Rom. 11:36). Nothing but God explains the song's existence.

This is but shorthand for speaking about God's creative generosity and its expression in creation "out of" nothing. In this chapter we must consider the meaning of creation out of nothing by looking at its biblical basis and what it does and does not entail about the creative act, how God "sings." Then we will explore the significance of creation out of nothing for God's relation to creation. Finally, all of this helps us understand creation and creatures as gifts—not poor things but rich recipients of God's loving generosity.

The Beginning of Music: Creation out of Nothing

We may start with an initial distinction: The song is *from* God but not *out of* God. Strictly speaking, the song isn't "out of" anything. It just began. Creation out of nothing means that there is nothing out of which God creates, because God creates *all* things. It will be worthwhile to unpack this brief thought before looking in the following sections at what difference it makes for the Christian understanding of Creator and creatures.

God Created All Things

"In the beginning, God created the heavens and the earth" (Gen. 1:1). Scripture's opening words initiate a line of reflection that leads us to the idea of creation out of nothing. The phrase "the heavens and the earth" is shorthand for the whole of that reality created by God, not merely two parts of it. This same thought is expressed elsewhere when we hear that God created "all things." Consider John's Gospel, which echoes the opening of Genesis: "In the beginning was the Word, and the Word was with God, and the Word was God. He was in the beginning with God. All things were made through him, and without him was not any thing made that was made" (John 1:1–3; cf. Eph. 3:9). The Word here is the only begotten Son of God, Jesus Christ (John 1:14, 17). He is distinct from the Father ("the Word was with God") and yet one God with the Father ("the Word was God"). He is therefore the Creator of "all things," who is himself uncreated, so nothing exists unless it was "made through him" (John 1:3).

Paul teaches the same truth in a hymn about Jesus Christ's creative power: "For by him all things were created, in heaven and on earth, visible and invisible, whether thrones or dominions or rulers or authorities—all things were created through him and for him. And he is before all things, and in him all things hold together" (Col. 1:16–17). Note the repeated use of "all things": Jesus created *all things*, he is the one for and through whom *all things* were created, he is preeminent over *all things*, and he sustains *all things* in their existence. And the several prepositions—"by" him, "through" him, "for" him, etc.—emphasize here, as elsewhere, the cosmic reach of God's creative activity, touching everything that exists (Rom. 11:36; 1 Cor. 8:6). Nowhere does Scripture limit the scope of "all" in these statements. Therefore, "all things" refers to everything created by God, the "whole creation" (Rom. 8:22). God is thus responsible for the existence of all things, all creatures.[1]

Out of Nothing

It's a small step from "God created *all things*" to "God creates out of nothing."[2] At its most basic, "out of nothing" emphasizes

1. Hearing this, we might easily ask, "Then what about evil?" Christians have traditionally maintained that evil does not *exist*, strictly speaking. It's not really a *thing*. Evil is the result of an absence of some good that should be. It describes something real only because it is a deformity of some reality, some thing, and not because evil is itself a reality. This is also why evil is fundamentally irrational. Hence, Scripture often describes it in terms of an absence: "unrighteousness," "lawlessness," "impurity," "darkness." Further, see Andrew Davison, *Participation in God: A Study in Christian Doctrine and Metaphysics* (Cambridge University Press, 2019), 239–59.

2. Davison, *Participation in God*, 14–18.

how seriously Christians believe that "all" in "all things" really means *all*, and not merely *some*. Whenever we manufacture something, we make it "out of" something else: wood, plastic, marble, and so on. This is the only way we can conceive of artistic activity. When we start to talk about God creating all things, we fall back on this way of thinking and speaking, so we say God created all things out of, well, "nothing." Yet it makes no sense to make something "out of" nothing. Early critics seized this opportunity to mock Christians, since everyone knows that nothing comes from nothing. An empty pantry doesn't miraculously yield dinner, after all. Christians have been merrily undeterred, for we know we are speaking about something at once unique and impossible to conceive. In fact, creation "out of nothing" is more of a denial than it is something we can conceive in our minds. Since God made *all* the things, we deny that anything but God falls outside the reach of that "all."[3]

Now, when we deny that there is anything "out of which" God creates, the denial runs deep. We must thoroughly chase away all thoughts of nothing allowing for something. There are no exception clauses to the radical claim that nothing but God explains creation. Among the important denials Christians have traditionally made are the following: Creation is not a change that happens to some preexisting thing. Creation is not an event

3. Reckoning with the fact that *nothing* really means "nothing" is challenging. We might feel unsettled about this, because we are unable to imagine nothing. In one respect, our inability captures the difficulty: We are created "out of" nothing, but we've never known *no*thing because we've always been *some*thing. We can scarcely imagine "nothing," any more than a deep-sea creature can imagine what it's like to be wet. The unsightly anglerfish has no point of reference for "being wet," which would require a knowledge of what lies far beyond its reach: dry land. Matters are even more hopeless for us. Not only are we incapable of forming an idea of nothing; the whole point of stating "nothing" is to deny that there's anything of which we might form an idea! This difficulty tempts us to reign in the meaning of *nothing* so that it leaves room for something outside of its reach. Because if *nothing* doesn't quite mean "absolutely nothing," then God's creative act becomes more like human acts of craftsmanship. This in turn would make creation out of nothing much easier for us to imagine and understand. However, anything short of creation out of nothing simply doesn't fit with Scripture's teaching that God created *all things*.

that happens within a preexisting time or place. Creation is not something that happens within God (the way a baby forms within a mother's womb). And so forth. To the casual listener, these denials might sound fussy and overly technical—perhaps even removed from Scripture. But if we listen closely, these denials are simply ways of refusing to qualify *no*thing away so that it allows for, or subtly becomes, *some*thing. They keep "nothing" in the negation rather than the affirmation column. "See to it that you avoid thinking of *nothing* as being something."[4]

That said, it is no denial of creation out of nothing to acknowledge that God makes some creatures emerge out of others. For instance, Peter says, "The earth was formed out of water and through water by the word of God" (2 Pet. 3:5). God explicitly tells us that he "formed the man of dust from the ground" (Gen. 2:7). God is often portrayed as a potter shaping things from clay (Jer. 18:1–11; Rom. 9:20–21). The opening of the creation hymn says the earth was "without form and void," suggesting that God creates by forming and filling things that are already there in some sense (Gen. 1:2). None of these passages contradict the doctrine we are considering, nor are they exceptions to creation out of nothing. They're doing something different.

First, the water and the dust, the earth and the clay are all creatures. They belong to "all things" created out of nothing. God creates the watery depths (Prov. 8:24), the dry land (Ps. 95:5), and even the darkness (Isa. 45:7). When God is shaping or forming one thing out of another, he is working with materials he has already created. Scripture at times will mention God introducing these materials, while at other times it describes God shaping those materials. This alerts us to an

4. Augustine, *Homilies on the Gospel of John* 1.13 (trans. Edmund Hill, *WSA* I/12:48); cf. Aquinas, *Commentary on the Gospel of John* 1.2.83.

important distinction between God's direct and indirect forms of creating. God creates directly by instantly bringing forth materials, and this is the most proper meaning of creation "out of nothing," whereas God creates indirectly by using materials he has already brought forth.[5]

Second, Scripture speaks of God's indirect creating for the purpose of teaching us connections between things. When God forms certain creatures out of others, he creates an interdependent relation between them. By God's Word, the earth emerges from the gathering of waters together on the third day, so the earth depends on water to be fructified (Job 36:27–28; Pss. 1:3; 104:10–13; Eccl. 1:7). Adam is formed from the ground, so human life is agrarian life (Gen. 1:29; 2:15; 3:17–19). Eve is formed from Adam's side, so the two are "one flesh" in marriage (Gen. 2:24). In all these instances, God establishes relations of interdependence in which distinct creatures can come together for the sake of fruitfulness, relations that become frustrated after the human fall into sin (Gen. 2:16–19; cf. 6:13–17).

God Creates Differently

Creation out of nothing thus leads us to see how different God's artistry is from every other. God doesn't belong to a general class of artists. Creation isn't simply the first instance of creativity. God is an artist differently; he creates differently, sings differently. We may register this difference in two ways.

First, there is no occasion for God's artistry, no context into which he steps and performs his work. His singing is like no other, for "his word runs swiftly" (Ps. 147:15). God has no vocal cords to activate, no diaphragm that grows tired; there

5. Christian theologians thus speak of "immediate" (direct) and "mediate" (indirect) creation: Francis Turretin, *Institutes of Elenctic Theology*, trans. George Musgrave Giger, ed. James T. Dennison Jr., 3 vols. (P&R, 1992–1997), 5.1.6 (1:432).

are no empty spaces waiting for sounds waves to fill them.[6] When God "sings," creation instantaneously and effortlessly appears.

Second, then, God is the Creator and not a mere craftsman. He "does all that he pleases" (Ps. 115:3; cf. 135:6) because he is the Almighty and sovereign Lord over all things (Isa. 40:9–31; Jer. 10:10–16). There is no eternal stuff or material lying around alongside God that limits what he can do, the way materials dictate what an artist can do with them. Every artist must respect the possibilities and limitations of the materials he or she uses.[7] This is true of any art form and any material, no matter how proficient and brilliant an artist is. However, the case is very different with God, because he is not merely the greatest artist working with the greatest variety and expanse of materials. God is the Creator of all stuff and materials. "Before" the world, there was only God. He didn't stumble across a cosmic heap of intractable materials and think to create what he could with them. When God composed the song, he did not borrow anything from elsewhere; he did not use preexisting notes and time signatures. Instead,

> he spoke, and it came to be;
>   he commanded, and it stood firm. (Ps. 33:9)

The beginning of this song is the beginning of music itself.

---

6. Basil of Caesarea, *Homilies on the Hexaemeron* 2.7: "When we speak of a voice and a word and a command with reference to God, we mean the divine word, not a sound sent out through phonetic organs, nor air struck by the tongue, but we believe that the bent of His will is presented in the form of a command, because it is easily comprehended by those who are being instructed" (trans. Agnes Clare Way, FC 46:32); cf. Augustine, *The Literal Meaning of Genesis* 1.1.1–2.6 (*WSA* I/13:168–70).

7. Materials exercise a kind of analogous "causality" in this regard, which is why philosophers and theologians call them *material causes*. The material cause of Michelangelo's statue of David is marble, for instance, be*cause* the marble is the reason the statue is marble (and not bronze, say). Of course, Michelangelo had to decide to carve the statue out of marble, but once that decision was made, he had to work *with* the marble, navigating its challenges and opportunities. Creation out of nothing is the denial that creation has any material cause.

The Singer's Relation to the Song: Distinguishing Creator and Creatures

Those are the basics of creation out of nothing. Now we must dig a little deeper to grasp its significance. We begin by underlining something implicit in our reflection thus far: The song of creation is a solo, not a duet or a symphony with many instruments. God sings this song alone without any accompaniment. Obviously, his singing elicits our own liturgical response: "Sing to the LORD, all the earth!" (Ps. 96:1). But the response is not the call. Any suggestion to the contrary would require that creation emerges from God plus something else, some other reality that God works with or against. The biggest problem with this view is that it leads to pagan mythology. Anything that could limit God would be another god, making God but one deity among others. Consequently, God would be something less than the Creator, and the world would be something more than his creation. We may avoid such mistakes by registering two consequences of creation out of nothing: (1) the infinite distinction between Creator and creation and (2) how this leads us to a proper understanding of God's relation to creation.

The Creator's Distinction from Creatures

God's creative activity distinguishes him from all else because there is no other Creator. In the Old Testament the verb "create" is attributed only to God, since no one or nothing else creates.[8] God tells us through his prophet,

> I am the LORD, who made all things,
> who alone stretched out the heavens,
> who spread out the earth by myself. (Isa. 44:24; cf. 45:12)

8. For the grammatical details of the Hebrew, see Raymond C. Van Leeuwen, "bārā'," in *New International Dictionary of Old Testament Theology and Exegesis*, ed. Willem A. Van Gemeren, 5 vols. (Zondervan, 1997), 1:731–32.

Having established this, Scripture then attributes creation to the Father (Acts 4:24; 1 Cor. 8:6; Eph. 3:9; Heb. 1:2), the Son (John 1:3; Col. 1:15–17; Heb. 1:10), and the Holy Spirit (Job 26:13; Pss. 33:6; 104:30). The Father creates through the Son and by the Holy Spirit. Prepositions like *through* and *by* distinguish the persons, but not the creating activity. The Trinity acts indivisibly: There "are *not* three *associate* causes, nor three authors of creation, but one cause, one author of creation, one creator."[9] There is one Creator because one God creates by one and the same will, power, and essence. God does not use any instruments or intermediaries to help him create, because these other things are themselves creatures. When God "creates" anything, he does something no one else can do, for which reason sinners pray, "Create in me a clean heart, O God" (Ps. 51:10).

The book of Revelation testifies to God's sole agency in creation by contrasting the Trinity and the demonic forces of Babylon. The satanic powers—vividly portrayed as the dragon, the beasts, and the harlot—attempt to impose their own order on creation and make it in their image, effectively seeking to counterfeit God's creative work.[10] Weaving monotonous verses in the dark, they vainly suppose that the song is theirs. But these demonic impostors can only deform things that already exist. Hence, they are "destroyers of the earth," who "corrupt" it (Rev. 11:18; 19:2). Only God can create things, because he alone can introduce a thing's entire being—its substance and its form—into existence. Anyone else can "create" in only an analogous sense by re-forming or de-forming things that God has already formed by his Word and Spirit.

9. David Hollatz, *Examen theologicum acroamaticum* (Leipzig, 1763), I.III, q. 7 (353). On the Trinity's indivisible works, see Scott Swain, *The Trinity: An Introduction* (Crossway, 2020), 105–20.

10. Richard Bauckham, *The Theology of the Book of Revelation* (Cambridge University Press, 1993), 51–53.

Thus, God distinguishes himself from all false "gods" because he alone is the Creator. False gods, which are only "so-called gods" (1 Cor. 8:5), are all created in a twofold sense. On the one hand, these so-called gods are mere idols, and "an idol has no real existence" (1 Cor. 8:4). Idols are mere artifacts made by human craftsmen.

> For all the gods of the peoples are worthless idols,
> but the Lord made the heavens. (Ps. 96:5)

> An idol! A craftsman casts it,
> and a goldsmith overlays it with gold
> and casts for it silver chains. (Isa. 40:19)

On the other hand, idols represent something real and sinister, for these so-called gods are really demons. "What pagans sacrifice they offer to demons and not to God" (1 Cor. 10:20; cf. Ps. 106:37). Therefore, idolatry involves the worship of what are "no gods" (Deut. 32:17) but mere creatures (Rom. 1:25). Creation out of nothing highlights what is implicit in Scripture's polemic against idolatry: There is the one Creator and there are many creatures, but there is nothing in between. Creation out of nothing therefore confronts us with the relentless distinction between God and creation.

We must register this truth in all its force by speaking of the infinite, qualitative distinction between the Creator and the creature.

God differs *infinitely*. Normal distinctions draw boundaries around things to show how they are not identical, but the distinction between God and creation is not like this. God is not limited by anything, even by the distinction between Creator and creature. God is not identical to creation, but neither is he cordoned off from it. He is at once transcendent and immanent, removed from all things and present to their innermost being. "In him we live and move and have our being" (Acts 17:28).[11]

God also differs *qualitatively*. Quantitative differences are measured in terms of bigger and smaller or more and less, but God's distinction from creation is not measurable in this way. This means that the world adds nothing to God, that "God plus the world" is not something bigger and better than "God himself."[12] God measures the world, but not vice versa (Isa. 40:12–17). God would be no less good or glorious without creation than he is with it, because God cannot be part of something else. Furthermore, his qualitative distinction from all things means that God is not even one "kind" of being alongside other kinds. There is no general classification scheme embracing both God and creatures, as two instances of something more general, that would explain them both. God is only like himself (Isa. 40:25; 46:5), whereas creatures are resemblances and imitations of God in some respect. Hence, we can speak of both God and creatures as "beings" by analogy, since creatures imitate God by existing. This radical distinction between God and creation is axiomatic, with wide-ranging significance for everything from the incarnation to the relation between grace and freedom.[13]

The Creator's Relation to Creation

The distinction between Creator and creation that follows from creation out of nothing leads to an understanding of God's relation to the world as asymmetrical.[14] That is to say, this

11. John of Damascus, *On the Orthodox Faith* 13: "All things are far from God, not by place but by nature" (trans. Norman Russell, PPS 62:93).

12. Robert Sokolowski, *The God of Faith and Reason: Foundations of Christian Theology* (Catholic University of America Press, 1982), 1–10.

13. Robert Sokolowski, "Creation and Christian Understanding," in *Christian Faith and Human Understanding: Studies on the Eucharist, Trinity, and the Human Person* (Catholic University of America Press, 2006), 38–50.

14. On this asymmetry, see John Webster, "*Non ex aequo*: God's Relation to Creatures," in *God Without Measure*, vol. 1, *God and the Works of God* (Bloomsbury, 2016), 115–26.

relation is necessary for creation's existence but not necessary for God's. Such an understanding of God's relation to creation refuses to separate or confuse Creator and creature (Ps. 10:11; Isa. 29:15; Rom. 1:25). If God and creation are separated, the result is a godless world. If God and creation are confused with one another, we effectively have a world-as-god (or a world-dependent god). Sometimes these results are very similar. Even modern naturalistic atheism, which promotes a godless world, tends to identify some part of the material world as inscrutably godlike—something within the universe that has the final word. Consequently, it can be a thin line separating a godless world and a world that's god. Either way, one has denied the asymmetry between God and creatures. These errors resonate with Ancient Near Eastern and Greco-Roman forms of pagan religion familiar to the first audiences of the Old and New Testaments.

According to pagan thought, the divinity or the gods are component pieces of the world.[15] The deities might be the most powerful or important parts, but they are no more than links in the same metaphysical chain as creatures, parts of a larger whole. However, mere "gods" or divine beings in pagan religions are always measured by one another and by those beneath them. Mere gods mutually limit one another, with each having its own domain (war, fertility, agriculture, etc.). Naturally, they fight over territory and feud for glory and power. But they are also often limited by lower rungs of the cosmos. Since these deities are part of the same cosmic fabric as their worshipers, they may be manipulated by rituals or magic practices that pull on

15. See Yehezkel Kaufmann, *The Religion of Israel: From Its Beginnings to the Babylonian Exile*, trans. Moshe Greenberg (University of Chicago Press, 1960), 22–59; Sokolowski, *The God of Faith and Reason*, 12–19. This is, of course, inevitably schematic and reductive. Kaufmann's views have been criticized for several reasons, but his central contention remains valid: Scripture's understanding of God is unlike paganism in its refusal of any ontological continuity between Creator and creation.

the right threads. Idolatrous conceptions of divinity and of creation thus lead to superstition and false religion (Acts 17:22).

These superstitious practices rest on superstitions about the world and ourselves. In the Babylonian creation myth *Enuma Elish*, the storm god Marduk kills his dragon-mother Tiamat, forges the world from her remains, and makes humans from dirt mixed with the blood of her slain lover. As Joseph Ratzinger observes, all these images testify to a certain way of interpreting life and the world in which we live: "The world is actually the body of a dragon, and man has dragon's blood in him. There is something sinister lurking at the bottom of the world; deep inside of man lies something rebellious, something demonic, something evil."[16]

The creation hymn avoids all such drama, for God's is the only voice singing. Creation is not a battleground of the gods. We are not the spoils of war, slaves burdened with taming the primordial chaos that runs through everything down to our own souls. Admittedly, polytheism seems to rhyme with people's initial experience of the world.[17] We don't normally hear the song's harmony. Various forces seemingly work against one another: Hurricanes wipe out human habitations; late frosts in the early spring destroy budding plants; droughts in the summer kill crops; cancer eats away at precious life. The world can appear to be governed by different forces that aren't always on the same page, maybe even different gods with different agendas.

Our initial experience of the world is forgetful of the one true living God. Scripture therefore commands us to "remember" our Creator (Eccl. 12:1). The heavens and the earth, the waters, the sun and moon and stars, as well as every crop and creeping thing, are creatures of the triune God. We may not,

16. Joseph Ratzinger, *The Divine Project: Reflections on Creation and the Church* (Ignatius, 2023), 29.

17. Ratzinger, *The Divine Project*, 19.

therefore, go looking for a secondary, "dark" source alongside God from which come all the things in this world we find distasteful or difficult, or even things that are genuinely wicked.[18] No doubt, there is something sinister lurking about—because of sin. Creation now groans under the burden of dissonance (Rom. 8:20–22), but the dissonance is not the product of an original polyphony. In the beginning, everything was "very good," resonant with God's musicality (Gen. 1:31).

Since God is the only Creator, his relation to creation is asymmetrical, not reciprocal. Creation's relation to God is fundamental for its existence, whereas the reverse is not true. God would be no less fruitful and glorious without creation than he is with it. God could be God without the world. This thought is foreign to pagan religion, in which divinities must always belong to the fabric of the world they rule or make because they do not create out of nothing. They are not ultimately sovereign but dependent on forces outside them. Scripture tells us, on the contrary, that God "calls into existence the things that do not exist" (Rom. 4:17) and that he holds everything together in his Word (Col. 1:17; cf. John 1:3). God depends on nothing, but everything depends on his Word. Creation depends on God absolutely, "since the song lasts while the singer continues to sing."[19] So, too, creation's liturgical response will depend on him at every moment, for its very existence depends on the Creator's call.

The Creator's Generosity

Everything we have discussed in this chapter expresses the Creator's generosity. This is the heart of both creation out of noth-

18. Athanasius, *Contra Gentes* 6–7, in *Contra Gentes and De Incarnatione*, ed. and trans. Robert W. Thomson (Oxford University Press, 1971), 15–19.

19. Davison, *Participation in God*, 27.

ing and the asymmetry between God and creatures. Scripture discusses this asymmetry most often in terms of God giving to creatures rather than receiving. This is why God's relation to creation is not reciprocal, as if it were mutually beneficial to both parties. Since God is infinitely blessed and glorious in himself, he has nothing to gain in creation and everything to give. Hence, God gives to all "life and breath and everything" while not really getting anything in return (Acts 17:25). God has no need of our goods (Ps. 16:2). He does not even need our worship or our righteousness, for anything we bring him is something he has already given us. "What do you have that you did not receive?" (1 Cor. 4:7; cf. Ps. 50:10–11). Augustine comments, "No one would say that he had served the interests of a fountain by drinking from it, or that he had served the interests of a light by using it to see."[20]

God's creative generosity is the backdrop to the truths we have been considering. But it might not appear that way on first glance. Indeed, it might seem that God is withholding something from us, since what he communicates to us is "less" than what he communicates within himself (even though we've just seen how we cannot think of God in terms of more and less). We saw in the previous chapter how God's propensity to communicate his own goodness is satisfied eternally and internally within the triune musicality. Each of the divine persons possesses the divine goodness in its infinite fullness, whereas creatures do not. This does not mean, however, that God is miserly. On the contrary. What he communicates to creatures is a finite resemblance of his goodness, an imitation of it. And a finite resemblance *of God* makes a world of difference.

It is precisely because God creates with an infinite distinction between himself and us that we are given so much, for a

20. Augustine, *City of God* 10.5 (trans. William Babcock, *WSA* I/6:309).

finite resemblance of God's goodness is so bountiful that it gives creation its *own* reality, goodness, and causality.[21]

First, by communicating a finite resemblance of his goodness to creatures, God gives them their own reality in distinction from him. Since God's goodness is infinitely real and alive, its mere likeness brims with reality and life. God's infinite fullness does not thereby mean that everything else must be empty. It means that everything is empty apart from God, "who fills" (Eph. 1:23). Creatures are not nothing but something. They are realities, not figments of our imagination or of God's. God is pleased not to exist alone but to have creatures who exist in his presence.

Second, God gives to creatures their own intrinsic goodness and worth. God is not glorified by refusing all goodness and worthiness to others, as if creation were merely a theater for *God's* agency, an occasion for *God's* goodness to manifest itself. Rather, God is glorified in giving goodness and worth to other things. When we read that "God saw everything that he had made, and behold, it was very good" (Gen. 1:31), this is not a statement God makes about himself—nor is it a statement he ever revokes. God delights in other good things. God loses none of his goodness and forfeits none of his glory by giving creatures their own goodness. Like an infinite wellspring, God's fullness fills other things without diminishing itself.

Finally, God gives to creatures the good that is causality and, in some cases, life and agency as well. Some creatures, such as rocks, are inanimate and have no agency, while nevertheless exercising causality in some sense.[22] But animate

21. For what follows, see Hermann Volk, "Kreatürlichkeit," *Münchener Theologische Zeitschrift* 2 (1951): 197–210. See also Davison's discussion of "derived solidity" in *Participation in God*, 68–79.

22. Gisbertus Voetius, "De creatione, pars secunda" 3, in *Selectarum disputationum theologicarum*, 5 vols. (Utrecht, 1648), 1:575, says that even things like rocks can be

creatures—such as trees, beasts, angels, humans—all have life and therefore powers that God gave them to exercise. Creatures have their own agency distinct from God, but not independent of him. While God is sovereign over all things and governs them all for his glory, he does not do so by suppressing creaturely agency with his own. God mysteriously works within things, moving them to move themselves without compromising his own divine freedom or their own created freedom. "It is God who works in you, both to will and to work for his good pleasure" (Phil. 2:13).[23] Indeed, God even grants rational creatures the agency to turn away from him. And when they do, it is they who sin, not God—much as a symphony's composer is not responsible when a violinist misreads the music.

God therefore dignifies creatures with real existence, intrinsic worth, and genuine moral responsibility and freedom. These gifts are really given, but they must be received. That is, the creature's gratitude must answer the Creator's gratuity.[24] Minimally, this means we acknowledge that these gifts are inseparable from their giver. Our life, our dignity, our freedom all really belong to us, but we cannot have them on our own terms. We cannot possess them independently of God, for they are intrinsically oriented to him as their source and end. He gives us these resemblances of his own goodness that he might make us resemble him even more and that, having filled us once, he might fill us forevermore in eternal bliss. And so it is that we first receive these gifts by recognizing their orientation to God and to our neighbor, that we might resemble the fruitful love

causes in the minimal sense of "material causality." That is, they assert themselves when we work with them and make things out of them (cf. note 7, p. 67, above).

23. Since we do not have space to discuss the doctrine of providence, we leave further consideration of this mystery aside (cf. Aquinas, *Summa theologiae* I, q. 105, aa. 4–5).

24. Kenneth L. Schmitz, *The Gift: Creation* (Marquette University Press, 1982), 44–48. We will return to this subject in chapter 7.

at the root of God's creative generosity (Matt. 22:36–40). The Creator gives us our own voice so that we can rise up in song to resonate with his own musicality.

Conclusion

Creation out of nothing reflects Scripture's teaching about the Creator. God is immeasurable and everlasting, the alpha and omega, the beginning and end of all things, the everlasting and almighty. Therefore, creation out of nothing is not one among many possible ways God could have created, but the only way the one true living God creates. This is how God sings.

Now, the notion of singing implies the use of words. To say that God "sings" the creation is to say that God creates through his Word. This Word does not return to him "empty" (Isa. 55:11), because it is full of his intrinsic musicality, so it fills other things. Creation out of nothing tells us that everything comes from God's Word: He "spoke, and it came to be" (Ps. 33:9); "his word runs swiftly" (Ps. 147:15). We therefore have life from God's Word, not from ourselves. We are not our own. God's asymmetrical relation to creation reminds us that this Word, who is the source of our life, is nearer to us than we are to ourselves.[25] This good news also expresses God's generosity, for God gives himself to us in his Word. Daily God's Word comes to us on the wings of his Spirit so that God's grace is nearer to us than our sin; God's mercy is nearer to us than our misery; God's patience is nearer to us than our anger and fleeting emotions; God's wisdom is nearer to us than our foolishness; God's power is nearer to us than our weakness. This general truth about God's relation to creation takes on greater significance when we understand the Word who is the song's melody.

25. Cf. Augustine, *Confessions* 3.6.11 (*WSA* I/1:83).

4

The Song's Melody

Hearing and Receiving God's Creative Word

In the previous chapter, we saw how God sings the song of creation. He sings it alone and without borrowing from elsewhere, since his artistry is only like itself. Thus, God creates all things out of nothing, and he does so through his Word. Now remember, all this song business is just a metaphor. We can't press it too hard or it won't work. But if we hold on to it loosely, we can continue and ask, How is God's Word like creation's melody?

Broadly speaking, melody is that part of a song that binds everything together; it organizes various notes in a particular rhythm and order that makes them memorable. Melody may be only part of the song, but it is a central part. Similarly, the Creator's song revolves around its melody: the Word. All the song's supporting notes and sounds are meant to harmonize with him. Apart from their relation to him, creation's many parts would be chaotic noise, for there would be no order and harmony within them. To appreciate what this tells us about the creation, we will now consider what it means that God created all things through his Word. After an initial discussion of (1) creation through the Word, we will proceed to explore the significance this has for created things as (2) little "words" that are (3) meant to exist in harmony with the Word.

God Creates Through His Word

In the prologue to the Fourth Gospel, John writes that God creates through his Word: "In the beginning was the Word, and the Word was with God, and the Word was God. He was in the beginning with God. All things were made through him, and without him was not any thing made that was made. In him was life, and the life was the light of men" (John 1:1–4).[1] As the prologue continues, John identifies this creative Word with Jesus. The Word through whom God creates is also the Word who "became flesh" (John 1:14) and thereby "exegeted" the Father for us (John 1:18). Jesus Christ is the life-giving Word articulated in life-giving flesh and blood. Throughout the Gospels Jesus exercises the Creator's power and authority over disease, death, demons, and even the subhuman creation. He is the one through and for whom creation exists: "one Lord, Jesus Christ, through whom are all things and through whom we exist" (1 Cor. 8:6); "all things were created through him and for him" (Col. 1:16; cf. Heb. 2:10). Just as Jesus looked out over the stormy sea, so he looks over the whole creation and restores its harmony with his voice (Mark 4:35–41).

1. As commentators on John 1:3 in Christian tradition observe, Holy Scripture does not use prepositions like "through" or "by" to suggest any inferiority between the divine persons. After all, it can speak of the Father as the one "through whom all things exist" (Heb. 2:10 CSB) and "by whom you were called into the fellowship of his Son" (1 Cor. 1:9). Creation is therefore "through" the Father, Son, and Spirit as much as it is "from" or "by" them, because the three persons are one God (cf. Acts 17:28; Rom. 11:36; 1 Cor. 8:6; Col. 1:16). In the Gospel of John, creation "through" the Word highlights the unity and distinction of the Father and Son in creating. The name Word is what chiefly discloses the point we are considering.

Approaching these statements from two different angles will help us appreciate what they tell us about creation.

God Creates Through Speaking

First, creation through God's Word deepens our understanding of God *speaking* creation into existence. When Scripture tells us creation happens through God's "Word," it is pointing us to who is responsible for creation. According to the Gospel of John, Jesus is responsible for creation not because he is incarnate, but because he is the eternal Word.[2] John uses this title for Jesus with great care. The title "Word" (*logos*) in John invokes the theme of God's spoken word throughout the Old Testament, where it connects to God's creative power, revelation, judgment, and deliverance.[3] The Word who became flesh is therefore God's complete self-revelation, as well as the one who judges and redeems the world he created (John 1:14, 18; cf. 3:16–18; 5:22–24). These meanings are all at work. Yet "Word" also means an element of speech or reasoning, as well as "reason" itself. With that in mind, we can appreciate that John's Gospel opens the same way as Genesis: "In the beginning" (Gen. 1:1; John 1:1). John's invocation of the "Word" recalls God's rhythmic speech in the creation hymn where "God said" and the consequence was that "it was so."[4] What's going on here?

John the Evangelist is rereading the creation hymn after what has happened to him. He has heard, seen with his eyes, looked upon, and touched the Word in his glory, "glory as

2. For more context, see Steven J. Duby, *God in Himself: Scripture, Metaphysics, and the Task of Christian Theology*, Studies in Christian Doctrine and Scripture (IVP Academic, 2019), 132–87 (esp. 166–72); R. B. Jamieson and Tyler Wittman, *Biblical Reasoning: Christological and Trinitarian Rules for Exegesis* (Baker Academic, 2022), 126–52.

3. D. A. Carson, *The Gospel According to John*, The Pillar New Testament Commentary (Eerdmans, 1991), 115, citing Ps. 107:20; Isa. 9:8; 55:11; Jer. 1:4; Ezek. 33:7; etc.

4. Gen. 1:3, 6–7, 9, 11, 14–15, 20 (the only instance where there is no corresponding "and it was so"), 24, 26–30.

of the only begotten from the Father, full of grace and truth" (John 1:14 NASB 1995; cf. 1 John 1:1–2). When Jesus ascended into heaven, he sent the Holy Spirit upon John and the other apostles at Pentecost. John then wrote his Gospel under the inspiration of the Holy Spirit. As Jesus promised, the Spirit *reminded* John of all that Jesus "said," which embraces all that was written about him, happened to him, and done by him (John 14:26; cf. 2:22; 12:16). We might expect the Spirit to remind John only of things Jesus said and things that happened during his earthly ministry, but the Spirit takes him back to "the beginning" of all things. Creation is one of the things Jesus did. As John remembers the creation hymn in light of Christ, he understands "God's Word" to encompass everything "God said" across the six days.[5] What God creates is therefore intimately related to the Word God speaks.

> By the word of the LORD the heavens were made,
> and by the breath of his mouth all their host. (Ps. 33:6; cf. 148:5)

Rereading God's creative speech as the Word sheds light on otherwise odd features of the Genesis creation hymn. If we give it some thought, it is strange to read that God creates by "speaking" during the six days of creation.[6] This strangeness is meant to catch our attention. Ordinary speech takes time and energy, and it makes noise that echoes through space. Even written "speech" takes shape on materials like stone, parchment, and paper. God's speech cannot be speech in this sense, because

5. In this connection, see Aquinas, *Summa theologiae* I, q. 34, a. 3. Hence, as Edward W. Klink, *John*, Zondervan Exegetical Commentary on the New Testament (Zondervan Academic, 2016), 93–94, observes, the same Greek word (*egeneto*) is used for "was made" in John 1:3 and "it was so" (in *kai egeneto*) throughout Gen. 1 (LXX). Something similar occurs when Jesus rebukes the storm and waves, such that "there was" a great calm (Mark 4:39).

6. Basil of Caesarea, *Homilies on the Hexaemeron* 2.7 (FC 46:32); Augustine, *The Literal Meaning of Genesis* 1.1.1–2.6 (*WSA* I/13:168–70).

it is the reason for all time and space, energy and matter. So how should we understand it? According to John the Evangelist, it's like a riddle whose answer is found in Jesus. The Word who became flesh to save us also created us, knows everything about us (John 4:39), and can take us to our ultimate end because he is that end (John 17:24). He is Lord over all things—even the Sabbath (John 5:17) and death itself (John 11:43)—as only the Creator can be. If creation "was created with reason, wisdom, and understanding and has been arranged with complete order, then he who governs and ordered it can be none other than the Word of God."[7] God speaks creation into existence, so all of it is thoughtful, meaningful, and purposeful communication. Only by remembering the creation hymn like John does may we connect these dots, but they are there to connect.

Creation Is Spoken by God

Second, creation through God's Word deepens our understanding of creatures as *spoken* realities echoing the spoken God himself. As we just saw, God's speech during the six days of creation is an obscure reference to his Word, the eternal Son of the Father. This reminds us of God's musicality, his readiness for the song of creation. But it does so with a twist that tells us something important about God's creatures we might otherwise overlook. In ordinary acts of speech, words disclose the heart of their speaker (Matt. 15:18). The title "Word" for Jesus tells us that something like this is also true within God. The speaking God (the Father) and the spoken God (the Son, the Word) are distinct and yet also identical, because what the Father speaks in his Word is his essence, everything he is. The Father speaks from his "abundance" in such a way that he gives "all" that he is

7. Athanasius, *Contra Gentes* 40, in *Contra Gentes and De Incarnatione*, ed. and trans. Robert W. Thomson (Oxford University Press, 1971), 111.

(cf. Matt. 12:34; John 16:15). This is why the Son is the perfect communication of the Father within God's eternal life: true God of true God, not made or created, but begotten (John 1:18; 14:9). And for this reason, the Word reveals something important about everything that *is* made or created. Namely, the Word is the source, pattern, or archetype for all created resemblances to God's life, substantiality, truth, and goodness.[8] Life and light are communicated to creatures "through him" because life and light are first "in him," their inexhaustible source and pattern (John 1:4). Creation declares the glory of God because it echoes the Word who is "the radiance of the glory of God" (Heb. 1:3).[9]

There is an analogy between God's eternal speaking of the Word and his temporal speaking of creation through the Word. This analogy has two main consequences. First, spoken creatures echo the eternally spoken God. As the Father expresses all of himself in his eternal Word, similarly he expresses a created resemblance of himself when he speaks other things into existence through his Word. To understand what creatures are and how they flourish, we must hear them as words spoken through God's Word. Second, Jesus is the everlasting treasury or thesaurus for the meaning of the words that echo him (Ps. 119:89; Col. 2:3). The song's melody therefore defines its harmonies. It remains for us to consider these two consequences in greater detail.

---

8. Maximus the Confessor famously makes a similar thought central to his entire theology: The Word (*Logos*) expresses himself in all the words (*logoi*), which are the principles of what creatures are, how they develop in relation to others and to God, and so forth (*Ambiguum* 7.15–16). Other theologians talk of creatures as expressions of God's "ideas" for the things he creates, as when an artist builds a work of art according to a plan in his or her mind (e.g., Augustine, *Homilies on the Gospel of John* 1.17 [*WSA* I/12:52]). Gregory of Nyssa, *On the Six Days of Creation* 9, trans. Robin Orton, Fathers of the Church: Shorter Works (Catholic University of America Press, 2021), 55, says something similar: "Everything that comes into being according to order and wisdom is an individual direct utterance by God." See also Bonaventure, *Commentary on Ecclesiastes*, vol. 7 of *Works of St. Bonaventure* (Franciscan Institute, 2005), 115.

9. Martin Luther, *Lectures on Genesis*, chaps. 1–5 (*LW* 1:50): "The Son has in Himself not only the image of the Divine Majesty but also the image of all created things."

Hearing What God's Creative Word Speaks: The Wholeness of Creatures

Because God creates all things through his Word, creatures are like "words of God."[10] God's Word is so radiant and communicative that his mere echoes are words in their own right: things with meaning and order that disclose the mind of their divine speaker. By confessing creatures to be words spoken through the Word, the church thereby refuses to let any other "word" or "song" define the world and its inhabitants. Only Jesus defines reality. As the "Amen, the faithful and true witness," Jesus is himself the ultimate referent for all truth in God's creation (Rev. 3:14; cf. Isa. 65:16). Containing the meaning of all creation's words in himself, he knows what they are, what they're for, and how they measure up to the Creator's will for their existence and life. Since the truth of ourselves, our lives, and the world is something God speaks, we must receive it by listening for the Creator's meaning in the Creator's Word.

The first consequence of this for the doctrine of creation is that it leads us to understand what creatures are as "words"; namely, they are *whole realities*. Martin Luther notices that God's words in the creation hymn are not empty or cheap talk but fulsome things. God "speaks true and existent realities," and this encompasses everything he speaks: "Sun, moon, heaven, earth, Peter, Paul, I, you, etc.—we are all words of God."[11] Ordinary human speech is not creative in this way but merely reactive, assigning "names to objects which have already been created." Luther continues, "But the divine rule of language is different, namely: when He says: 'Sun, shine,' the sun is there at once and shines. Thus the words of God are realities, not bare words."[12]

10. Luther, *Lectures on Genesis*, chaps. 1–5 (*LW* 1:47).
11. Luther, *Lectures on Genesis*, chaps. 1–5 (*LW* 1:21).
12. Luther, *Lectures on Genesis*, chaps. 1–5 (*LW* 1:22).

Now, since creatures are not bare words, but fulsome realities, they must be understood as *wholes*. Bracketing part of a creature from the whole is like bracketing part of a word from the rest of it. The letters *t-o-p* are part of *stop*, but they mean something else entirely without the *s* or if arranged differently (*p-o-t*). What creatures are, they are as the whole, ordered words that God speaks through his Word.[13] This is the way they express their Maker's meaning. This meaning involves what we may call the created order. The "whole" picture of what creatures are involves not only the individual creature's nature (including body and, where applicable, soul) but also creatures' relations to one another and to God (their contours throughout time and space). Every creature possesses some such wholeness. For our purposes, we will consider the wholeness of creatures vertically and horizontally, with a focus on human creatures.

The Vertical Axis of Wholeness

The first aspect of creaturely wholeness is vertical, the creature's relation to its Creator. If we bracket the creature from the Creator, we lose the ability to see it as a "creature," and therefore we lose sight of the source of its dignity, value, purpose, and meaning. As created words, creatures don't mean just anything we want them to mean. They are invested with a meaning and purpose that can be fulfilled only by glorifying the Creator who spoke them in the first place. Creatures' relation to their Creator reminds us that no creature can serve the role of God, nor can creatures be divorced from his sovereign dominion over them. This is something that everyone implicitly recognizes. We know we are not responsible for the existence of things. Someone else is. Even creatures like the sun, moon, and stars

13. On the importance of this for ethics, see Oliver O'Donovan, *Resurrection and Moral Order: An Outline for Evangelical Ethics*, 2nd ed. (Eerdmans, 1994), 85–91.

point beyond themselves to their Creator (Ps. 19:1–3).[14] In this respect, they anticipate the apostles, who point to Christ (Rom. 10:18). And though we may turn our ears from it, this testimony has a musical character:

> Their music goes out through all the earth,
> their words reach to the end of the world.
> (Ps. 19:4 NEB)

Suppressing this knowledge—and the language of "suppressing" suggests it's already known to some extent—is a morally culpable form of ignorance that leads to idolatry (Rom. 1:20). Where we ignore that the things of this world are creatures of the Creator, we either invest them with the weightiness and splendor they cannot bear (Rom. 1:23), or ignore the ends and purposes for which the Creator made them (Rom. 1:26–27). Idolatry thus leads us to misuse other creatures and even our own bodies for our own pleasure, rather than God's good pleasure. It leads us to conceive of our days and relations to others as serving our glory, rather than God's.

The Horizontal Axis of Wholeness

We may also consider the wholeness of a creature horizontally, in relation to itself and other creatures. In relation to itself, creatures are inseparable from the bodies and souls God gives them, as well as the specific ways they inhabit time and space. All these factors give "shape" to the creature's wholeness. When God creates a human person, for example, he creates him or her as a whole composite of a sexually dimorphic body and soul (Gen. 1:27; Ps. 139:13–15), a whole temporal lifespan complete with a beginning and an end that he establishes (Ps. 139:16),

14. Origen, *Contra Celsum* 5.12–13; Augustine, *Expositions of the Psalms* 148.3 (*WSA* III/20:561); Basil, *Homilies on the Hexaemeron* 3.9 (FC 46:52–53).

a whole set of spatial relationships to local places within the world, family, and neighbors (Acts 17:26). This overall shape of our creatureliness describes what and who we are in all our particularity.

That said, we do not belong to any of these parts of our wholeness. None of these aspects of the creature are absolute, for the whole creature and all its parts belong to God. He may require people to leave their homeland, their family, and their friends (Gen. 12:1; Luke 14:26), to forego some of the goods available to the body and soul (Matt. 19:12; 2 Cor. 12:7), or to live shorter or longer than they would choose (Matt. 26:39; Heb. 11:32–38). Jesus himself displays a royal freedom from all these relationships, since none of them command absolute allegiance.[15] The kingdom of God relativizes many of these goods with greater goods without negating them as goods.[16] Grace perfects but does not destroy nature. Our wholeness within these horizontal aspects is not something from which we may divorce ourselves, but neither is it something to which we may reduce ourselves. The horizontal and vertical dimensions of creatures are inseparable.

Demonic forces, on the other hand, seek to destroy nature and grace, to divorce all these vertical and horizontal aspects of

---

15. For further detail, see Karl Barth, *Church Dogmatics*, 4/2, ed. G. W. Bromiley and T. F. Torrance, trans. G. W. Bromiley (T&T Clark, 1936), 171–80; O'Donovan, *Resurrection and Moral Order*, 93–97. The notion of creation's "order" has sometimes been abused (as in 1930s Germany) on the assumption that current conditions of the created world, such as ethnic disparities and national identities, were immutable laws of creation's order. This became the pretext for arguing, for example, that churches segregated by ethnic or national differences are thereby upholding God's created order, however else Christ may reconcile those differences in his body (cf. Eph. 2:14). These distortions are foreign to Scripture and the understanding of created order that has predominated throughout Christian tradition. For an assessment of some such arguments, see Ryan Tafilowski, "A Reappraisal of the Orders of Creation," *Lutheran Quarterly* 31, no. 3 (2017): 288–309; and for some historical context, see Robert P. Ericksen, *Theologians Under Hitler: Gerhard Kittel, Paul Althaus, and Emanuel Hirsch* (Yale University Press, 1985), 79–119.

16. It is here that Christian tradition reflects on the order of love (*ordo amoris*) within our relationships to these various goods. For some orientation, see James R. Wood, "Ordering Our Social Lives," *Ad Fontes*, October 26, 2023, https://adfontesjournal.com/.

our wholeness. Just as Satan despises God's spoken word and tries to uproot it wherever it is sown (Mark 4:15), so he rages against God's created order in overt and covert ways. Demons always work to rip apart what God joins together as whole realities, fracturing God's creatures. They tear asunder body and soul, sex and marriage, husband and wife, created goods and gratitude (Mark 5:1–20; 1 Cor. 7:1–5; 10:1–22). They also seek to confuse what God distinguishes, presenting a false conception of reality, shorn of the fruitfulness and wholeness God intends (Gen. 6:1–4; Rom. 1:24–25). This drives the fall narrative from Genesis 3–11, in which sin and its consequences mix all manner of things God separated at creation.[17] Unclean spirits therefore seek confusion about the integral relationship between such things as humans and other animals, soul and body, man and woman, people and place, Creator and creature, and especially Christ and his church.[18] Avoiding this confusion requires us to listen attentively to God's creative speech.

Hearing the Whole Word God Speaks About Us

Creation through God's Word reminds us that nothing God says about a creature is incidental to its reality, a negotiable "part" we can bracket from something truer and more fundamental. God does not speak partial, divided realities into existence, because his word is not a partial, divided thing. He does not speak hypocritically, saying one thing and meaning another (2 Cor. 1:17–20). God's word is simple, making those who adhere to it simple and "whole" (Ps. 119:9–10). "What therefore God has

17. See, again, L. Michael Morales, *Who Shall Ascend the Mountain of the Lord? A Biblical Theology of the Book of Leviticus*, NSBT 37 (IVP Academic, 2015), 51–74; Edward W. Klink III, *The Beginning and End of All Things: A Biblical Theology of Creation and New Creation*, Essential Studies in Biblical Theology (IVP Academic, 2023), 54–66.

18. The list could go on to include such things as appearances and reality, goodness and being, and more.

joined together" in his creative speech "let not man separate" (Mark 10:9). A few examples will illustrate the truth and point to some of the ways we are tempted to resist it.

First, God is not double-minded when he speaks humans into existence as whole things comprising both body and soul. The souls of human creatures are not more real than their bodies, and bodies are not extrinsic accessories to some "true self." The body is the natural expression of the soul. Conversely, the soul expresses itself in the body naturally. The two go together as a whole.[19] Someone's soul gives his or her body *these* particular powers in *this* particular arrangement. The body is therefore the soul's instrument for glorifying God, not its experimental laboratory for demonic delusions (1 Cor. 3:16–17; 6:15–20). Sin and disorder leave us thinking otherwise: My body is essentially bad and something to be rejected; my body doesn't express the "real me," so I must redesign it; my fulfillment and meaning can come only from misusing my body contrary to God's creative speech. All such deceit leads to dissonance.

Second, God is not dissembling when he tells us which kinds of actions are "natural" and which are not (Rom. 1:26). Here, too, God has the whole creature in view: the unity of the creature's nature and its enactment in relations, conduct, and life. God knows the whole creature in relation to himself, since he is its source and end. So, when God's word elicits acts from us, they aim at the full flourishing of our natures, the attainment of the ends to which he orders us. This looks different for a whale than it does for a human. But in both cases, God determines the nature and thus the whole temporal and spatial shape of its life.

In this same vein, the nature of a thing derives from the distinctions God draws between creatures. The distinction between

19. Aquinas, *Summa theologiae* I, q. 76, a. 1; Joseph Ratzinger, *Eschatology: Death and Eternal Life*, 2nd ed., trans. Michael Waldstein (Catholic University of America Press, 1988), 146–50.

man and woman, for example, is something taught by "nature itself" (1 Cor. 11:14).[20] The ways men and women dress, speak, and carry themselves differ from one culture to another. And Scripture presents no single culture, or isolated period of a culture, as the standard-bearer for every culture. But all cultures must respect this distinction rather than blur it. Whether through technology, artifice, or perverse custom, contemporary Western society embodies a demonic suspicion of this distinction, as if it were repressive: "Did God actually say . . . ?" (Gen. 3:1). Yet God speaks and preserves this distinction as something good. Our wholeness as men and women in the Word includes this distinction for the sake of our mutual life and fruitfulness (1 Cor. 11:11–12). The church is itself a sign of this (Eph. 5:32). Again, demonic forces rage against the diversity and distinction of God's creation, pursuing monotonous noise rather than song.

Last, God's Word is eternal, not momentary, so he holds the whole of our time in himself.

> Forever, O Lord, your word
> is firmly fixed in the heavens. (Ps. 119:89)

> In your book were written, every one of them,
> the days that were formed for me,
> when as yet there was none of them. (Ps. 139:16)

We may not, therefore, separate our days from their wholeness in God's eternal Word. This became an acute temptation with the rise of psychoanalysis and therapeutic culture, which promote methods of identifying the "true" self with one's past and therefore with a part of life's temporal arc.[21] This becomes

20. John Calvin, *Commentary on 1 Corinthians* 11:12 (CO 49:478), recognizes that by "nature" here Paul has in view the way nature is expressed in particular "mores," the customs and conventions of a particular culture.

21. Cf. Eva Illouz, *Cold Intimacies: The Making of Emotional Capitalism* (Polity, 2007), 7.

a demonic form of (mis)remembrance that fixates on discovering who we are in something other than God's Word. Again, since God alone knows our days, we should not presumptuously try to predict the future or agonize over what tomorrow holds (Eccl. 3:11; Matt. 6:34; James 4:13–15). Instead, we are to entrust ourselves to God in patience (Eccl. 12:13–14). Jesus is God's unvacillating Word, God's *yes* and *amen*, that our time is not merely one arbitrary minute stacked upon another. Since Christ gathers them under his wings, our days and years are hastening toward an end whose weight and significance are not worth comparing with our present struggles (Rom. 8:18). Like the truth of creation itself, this is something we know only by faith, trusting the Word through whom all things are arranged to set our lives straight. However difficult it may be at times, faith in God's invisible Word enables us to confess:

> Those who sow in tears
>   shall reap with shouts of joy!
> He who goes out weeping,
>   bearing the seed for sowing,
> shall come home with shouts of joy,
>   bringing his sheaves with him. (Ps. 126:5–6)

In the heavenly, imperishable city Christ is bringing us, griefs will give way to glory, and prayers to praise. "Toil and groaning will disappear; supplications will fade and songs of praise take their place."[22]

We cannot speak our own truth into existence. Our words are too powerless, empty, and divided to define reality (Rom. 3:4). Jesus tells us the truth about creatures because he *is* the truth

22. Augustine, *Expositions of the Psalms* 86.9 (trans. Maria Boulding, *WSA* III/18:255).

(John 14:6). He therefore gives us rest from our anxious attempts to find the truth apart from him (Matt. 11:29).

Responding to God's Creative Word: The Harmony of Creatures

Hearing God's creative word about what we are also involves a response: obedience. We must receive the Word's instruction about what we are, but we must also respond with all that we are (Deut. 6:4–5). God's word is near us, but we must welcome it into our hearts and our mouths (Deut. 30:14; Rom. 10:8). Rather than resisting what God's word says about us, we must be conformed to it so that we "may discern what is the will of God, what is good and acceptable and perfect" (Rom. 12:2). The song's melody must find its home in our souls so that we express it on our lips.

The second consequence of God creating all things through his Word therefore follows from the wholeness of creatures, for it concerns the way that wholeness finds expression in life. Augustine voices this in terms of worship: "When you praise God, praise him with your whole selves: let your voice sing, let your life sing, let your actions sing."[23] Creatures are words meant to reverberate with the Word. Their voices are meant to harmonize with the song's melody. Christian tradition often appeals to the metaphor of "harmony" to describe how creatures flourish within God's created order, enacting their natures in accord with God's will and creation's order.[24] Harmony therefore overlaps with biblical themes like rest, righteousness, purity, and peace. It describes creatures as they resonate more and

---

23. Augustine, *Expositions of the Psalms* 148.2 (Boulding, *WSA* III/20:561).

24. For an overview of this theme in the early church, see Everett Ferguson, "Toward a Patristic Theology of Music," in *Studia Patristica*, vol. 24, *Historica, Theologica et Philosophica, Gnostica*, ed. Elizabeth A. Livingstone (Peeters, 1993), 266–83; Doru Costache, *Humankind and the Cosmos: Early Christian Representations* (Brill, 2021), 61–108.

more with God's will for their lives, as they are characterized by fruitful love, God's musicality (1 John 4:7–12). A melody might exist without harmony just as God might exist without creatures, but harmony depends upon melody.[25] There is an asymmetry because melody shapes harmony. So, too, the Word shapes all creation's words by his Spirit so that they might agree with his melody. We may grasp the significance of this by looking at (1) how God forms what God speaks and (2) how this formative work imparts harmony to creatures, tuning them to glorify the Father through the Word and by the Spirit.

God Forms What God Speaks

Created life is necessarily related to God's Word and Spirit as its source and wellspring. Hints of this already permeate the creation hymn. When God "created the heavens and the earth," he did so in an initially unformed state: "The earth was without form and void" (Gen. 1:2). At this point early in the hymn, the Spirit was brooding over the unformed mass, waiting for the Word to be spoken over the creation like a seed from which he would bring forth fruit (Job 26:13; 33:4; Ps. 33:6). We have not yet read that "God said" anything. Rather, God began to speak as he formed and filled his creation throughout the six days: "And God said . . ." (Gen. 1:3–31). The creation hymn thus guides listeners from creation's unformed state to its formed state, and the decisive difference is God's Word, who makes things good and beautiful by his Spirit.

We learn more about this formative work through the gospel. As God brought life out of nothing and light out of darkness, so the Word who is Jesus brings life and light into a world deformed by death and blindness (John 5:26; Rev. 22:5). Hence, "in him was life," but not in the sense that it is no longer there,

25. Victor Zuckerkandl, *The Sense of Music* (Princeton University Press, 1959), 173.

because he was and is "the life" (John 1:4; 14:6). Light and life remain in the Word, even if they disappear from the world. The Word in whom life resides comes to his creation wrecked by death so that his people "may have life and have it abundantly" (John 10:10; 11:25). From the fact that Jesus gives eternal life (John 3:16–17; 6:32–58), we remember that the Word was and remains the source of all life and light. "It is He who sustains the life of every living thing, and Who gives spiritual life to all reason-endowed creatures. He is light—not light perceivable by the senses, but . . . light that enlightens the soul."[26] It is only in turning to him that things will find life and harmony.[27]

Notably, the Word who does all this is first described as being "with God" or, we could say, turned "toward God" (John 1:1).[28] This is his eternal harmony within God's musicality, as the radiance of the Father's glory in all he is and does (John 5:19; Heb. 1:3). The Son's harmony is also described as his existing in the Father's bosom and abiding in the Father (John 1:18; 15:5). So, too, Jesus wants his disciples to rest in his bosom and abide in him like branches in a vine (John 12:24; 15:4–7). He returns from the world to the Father to prepare a place for his followers (John 14:1–3; 16:28). If they abide in him, he will abide in them and they will adhere to the Father in him (John 14:23). That is, they will share his harmony, his filial intimacy with the Father. This is the harmony the Son wants to impress upon his people (John 15:11; 17:24), and he does so

26. Theophylact of Ohrid, *The Explanation of the Holy Gospel According to John*, trans. Christopher Shade (Chrysostom, 2007), 15.

27. Augustine, *The Literal Meaning of Genesis* 1.4.9 (trans. Edmund Hill, *WSA* I/13:171): "By . . . being formed creation imitates, every element in its own way, God the Word, that is the Son of God who always adheres to the Father in complete likeness and equality of being, by which he and the Father are one; but it does not imitate this form of the Word if it turns away from the creator and remains formless and imperfect, incomplete."

28. The phrase *pros ton theon* can mean "toward God" but is usually translated as "with God" (John 1:1). Either translation is plausible, since both underscore the unique intimacy between the Son and the Father (cf. Luke 15:18–20).

by forming them as he formed all things in the beginning.[29] As disciples are conformed to Christ, they resonate with his own harmony the more they resemble God's goodness not only in their existence but in their *life*, in all their conduct and relations to God and neighbor.

God Forms Harmony with His Word and Spirit

Jesus is harmony in himself, the radiance of God's glory, the revelation of God's fruitful life of love. He therefore forms creatures for harmony. But just what is this "harmony" that God forms in us? Sticking with the example of human creatures, we may now appreciate what created harmony is. Before sin, harmony characterized the relation between the soul and the body and the working of the soul's powers.[30] The mind, will, and affections all worked in concert, properly ordered to God and governed by his Word. After turning away from the Word, Adam and Eve lost this concord within themselves and fell into disorder: the body and soul often at odds, the soul's powers pulled in contrary directions, their relations to God and to one another compromised by fear and pride.

The Word therefore assumed our flesh as his "instrument" or organ by which he rendered to God the response of human harmony we failed to offer.[31] Now, by his Spirit, he instills

29. Paul thus uses language of *form*ing, con*form*ity, and trans*form*ation to describe how the Spirit imparts Christ's harmony to his disciples (Rom. 8:29; Gal. 4:19; cf. Phil. 2:7; 3:21). This extends a pattern throughout the Old Testament, where "forming" describes God's works of creation (Pss. 94:9; 95:5; 139:16; Isa. 43:7) and redemption (Isa. 43:1; 44:2, 24).

30. Francis Turretin, *Institutes of Elenctic Theology*, trans. George Musgrave Giger, ed. James T. Dennison Jr., 3 vols. (P&R, 1992–1997), 5.10.8 (1:466), speaks of humanity's original righteousness before sin as "a harmony," such that the body obeys "the affections, the affections the will, the will reason, reason the divine law." See also Athanasius, *Contra Gentes* 31.

31. Cyril of Alexandria, *Scholia on the Incarnation of the Only Begotten* 25, in John McGuckin, *St. Cyril of Alexandria: The Christological Controversy, Its History, Theology, and Texts* (Brill, 1994), 320: "The body was made his very own through a true union and thus served the function of an instrument."

the fruits of this harmony, tuning our hearts to sing his praise. With a sovereign summons, he calls forth consonance from dissonance, light from darkness, and life from death: "Come out" (John 11:43; cf. 1 Pet. 2:9). Paul thus parallels God's transformation and renewal of our minds with our ability to offer worship that is "reasonable" (*logikos*), or Word-like (Rom. 12:1–2). God's Word summons us to life and thereby forms us. As we are conformed to the Word's own servant "form," his adhering to the Father in wholehearted love (Phil. 2:7), our lives are reordered to creation's doxological end. Just so, we are freed for further forms of harmony that can characterize our relations to other people in civic and especially church life, and finally between us and the subhuman creation.[32] The life that the Spirit gives us shapes us with Christ's freedom to serve his Father (Rom. 8:2; 2 Cor. 3:17; Gal. 5:1).

The song's notes must be governed by the song's melody, the Word. Jesus therefore reconciles the world to himself so that its discordant notes and digressions may rest in him. The gospel is a window into the Word's formative work in creation, for he is the inexhaustible source of creatures' wholeness and their harmony, their full flourishing as the creatures he has made them to be. While only humans bear God's image, creation as a whole and in all its parts bears traces of the Creator's musicality because it is his song. And so all creatures individually and together find their forms of harmony in submission to the Word.

Athanasius thus comments: "By obedience to this Word of God things on earth receive life and things in heaven subsist. Through him all the sea and the great ocean keep their movement within their proper limits, and all the dry land is covered with verdure in all kinds of different plants."[33] The Word tunes

32. For a particularly insightful sociological analysis of what such harmony looks like, see Hartmut Rosa, *The Uncontrollability of the World* (Polity, 2020).

33. Athanasius, *Contra Gentes* 42 (Thomson, 117).

the world like a musician playing a harp, "skillfully combining the bass and the sharp notes, the middle and the others," so that "through him a wonderful and truly divine harmony is produced."[34] All the song's parts are meant to reverberate with the Word who forms them as various likenesses of his own goodness, life, and fruitfulness. The Word's power to bring peace and rest to the natural world is an analogy for what he does in the human heart (Mark 4:39).[35]

We shall explore the significance of this created harmony further in the next chapter. For the moment, it's enough to see that what God intends for creatures to be he intends in and through his Word, by his Spirit. The Word, who perfectly adheres to the Father, who rests in the Father's love, now summons his listeners to resound with that harmony, which lets the Creator's love define the existence and life of them and all other things.

Having said this, we must recognize that the harmonious glory all things are meant to reflect is not yet an object of sight, but only of faith and hope (Rev. 21:23). While all created words enjoy the wholeness God speaks for them, existing within his created order, they do not all enjoy the full harmony to which God summons them. When John says, "What we will be has not yet appeared," he speaks of a redemptive reality that resonates in the created order as well (1 John 3:2). For no creature may say that what it is exhausts its meaning, nor that its meaning characterizes it entirely yet.[36] What something is in its wholeness belongs to its meaning, to God's will for it, but it still awaits the completion of this meaning in the living of its

34. Athanasius, *Contra Gentes* 42 (Thomson, 117, 119).

35. See Augustine, *Sermons* 63 (*WSA* III/3:173–74).

36. Hermann Volk, "Kreatürlichkeit," *Münchener Theologische Zeitschrift* 2 (1951): 202: "For the meaning of creaturely essence to be fulfilled, something must come to it that is not itself the essence. . . . That is why every creature is not perfect in itself; it is needy, oriented towards the meaningful fulfillment of its being, not somewhere, but in God, in whom alone essence equals meaning."

life before God who consummates all things. The Word is still "working" harmony within things (John 5:17). Creation therefore still awaits the Word's judgment, his shaking of all things so that only harmony remains (Heb. 12:25–29).

Conclusion

Creation through the Word means that Christ both is responsible for creation and stands at its center. He is the mediator of all things, not only salvation, truth, and judgment but also life itself (John 1:14; 5:26).[37] Just as John reinterpreted the creation hymn in light of Christ, we must "remember" creation through the Word in light of salvation through the Word. Jesus is the Creator because only the one who is the beginning as Creator can also be the beginning as the Savior, "the firstborn from the dead" (Col. 1:18). As the Spirit leads us into the truth found in Christ, he reminds us of what we are prone to forget: that we are creatures of the Word, meant to exist in harmony with the song's melody. He also convicts us of how short we fall of this truth, for we have split apart what God makes whole and sown discord where God intends concord. Yet, by bringing us to the Word, the Spirit brings the Word to us and thereby renews within us the opportunity for song, our nature as creatures.

37. On the important difference between Christ's mediation of salvation and creation, see Daniel J. Treier, *Lord Jesus Christ* (Zondervan, 2023), 93–101. It is specifically on account of his human nature that Christ is the mediator of salvation (1 Tim. 2:5; Heb. 9:15). That said, we can also understand "mediation" in a broad sense to mean that all communication from God the Father comes *through* the Son, *by* the Spirit. Therefore, Christ is a mediator according to both natures (cf. Turretin, *Institutes of Elenctic Theology*, 14.2 [2:379–84]). His mediatorial work is possible only on account of the divine power permeating his human activity, doing human things divinely and divine things humanly (cf. Maximus, *Ambiguum* 5.26).

5

The Frustrated Orchestra

Humans and Other Creatures

Praise God from whom all blessings flow;
Praise Him all creatures here below;
Praise Him above ye heav'nly host;
Praise Father, Son, and Holy Ghost.
Amen.

This doxology, originally written by the Anglican Bishop Thomas Ken and sung by many Christian churches around the world, summons all creation to a cosmic liturgy of praise. The theme is deeply biblical.[1] The concluding words of the Psalter perhaps do not surprise us: "Let everything that has breath

1. God makes "the going out of the morning and the evening to shout for joy" (Ps. 65:8). As God fructifies the earth, it responds in song: "The pastures of the wilderness overflow, / the hills gird themselves with joy, / the meadows clothe themselves with flocks, / the valleys deck themselves with grain, / they shout and sing together for joy" (Ps. 65:12–13; cf. 89:12; Isa. 55:12). Again: "Let heaven and earth praise him, / the seas and everything that moves in them" (Ps. 69:34). The "trees of the forest sing for joy / before the LORD" (Ps. 96:12–13).

praise the LORD" (Ps. 150:6). But we might not expect to hear this call extended even to things that have neither breath nor life. In Psalm 148, the leader calls upon the heavens, skies, earth, and sea, and all that populates them—including angels, sea creatures, mountains and trees, animals, even elements and natural forces—to "praise the LORD" (Ps. 148:1). Just as God created "all things," so all things are summoned into the cosmic liturgy of praise.

Our consideration of creation as God's song must therefore consider the liturgical response of all God's creatures, humans included. Here we come face to face with the orchestra or choir that meets God's song with created song. We cannot understand our own purpose as creation's liturgists without considering the creatures we are supposed to lead. Our praise is bound up with other creatures because so are our lives and our failures. For our purposes, we must consider three things: (1) the shape of created life as an opportunity for song, (2) the orchestra of all creation under the leadership of humanity, and finally (3) the vanity or futility creation suffers from the failures of its liturgists.

The Opportunity to Sing: The Shape of Created Life

In previous chapters we have seen several things about created life, such as its giftedness, contingency, reality, goodness, and (in some cases) agency. We have also discussed its formation by God's Word as something whole that is meant to resound with the Word, like the harmony of notes with a song's melody. All these qualities speak to the fact that created life is the opportunity to sing the Creator's praise: "I will praise the LORD as long as I live" (Ps. 146:2).

Insofar as created life is an opportunity for praise, it concerns the (1) doxological community of humans and other creatures, as well as (2) their common glorification of the Creator. We may consider each of these in turn.

The Doxological Community of Creation

The opportunity to sing is a shared opportunity.[2] Every creature is absolutely dependent on God and relatively dependent on other creatures. This complex web of mutually dependent relationships constitutes part of creation's natural "harmony," the coexistence of things according to the good functioning of their natures. We may appreciate this with the example of human life, and with good reason. Humans have spirit, like the angels; bodies, like the animals; and nutritive functions for growth, like vegetable life. So humanity is like a small portrait of all created life. For as we see in ourselves, created life comes to us *through* others and therefore *with* others.

First, God gives us created life through and with other human life. Anyone who doubts this should consult his or her belly button. Genealogically, our lives come to us as God blesses the procreative union of a biological mother and father, the joining together of two distinct elements from opposite sexes (Pss. 113:9; 127:3).[3] Scripture thus speaks of the "generations" (*toledot*) of people, referring to genealogical relations, including ancestors, as well as descendants (e.g., Gen. 5:1; 6:9; 10:1). Human life is a window into all created life in the sense that it is born out of things that precede it, and it has the potential for further births. Here as elsewhere, we see God's creative purpose of fruitfully joining together things that are kept

2. This section expands on the "horizontal axis" of creaturely wholeness from chap. 4 (p. 87).

3. Ephraim Radner, *A Time to Keep: Theology, Mortality, and the Shape of a Human Life* (Baylor University Press, 2016), 53–63, and elsewhere, describes created life as "filiated," how its thick texture is found in the bonds between family and community, being anchored thereby in something other than an individual's will. The "generation" observations are inspired by Jean-Pierre Sonnet, "Generare, perché?" Una prospettiva biblica," *Anthropotes* 36 (2020): 139–90.

distinct, like the two human sexes.[4] Every human life has a genealogy, which is one of Scripture's preferred ways of narrating both history and the interrelatedness of human life. This is why the narration of history begins in Genesis with a "genealogy" and why its culmination begins with Jesus's genealogy, tying his life to Israel's and to God's life-giving purposes (Gen. 2:4; Matt. 1:1). Our lives are therefore given to us through others and in relation to others, but ultimately from God. Ephraim Radner notes how this means that my life is defined by God's gift rather than whether anyone else, myself included, finds my life desirable.[5]

Scripture also speaks of a "generation" (*dor*) in the sense of a group of people who exist at the same time and place, and who are united in some sense for better or worse (Gen. 6:9; 7:1). In this respect, the created life God gives overlaps the life he gives to others (Acts 17:26–28). Created life is meant to be lived with others in communities, friendships, and families, all of which come with responsibilities stretching out behind us, around us, and before us (Ex. 20:5). The second table of the law especially is concerned with these responsibilities (Deut. 5:16–21). Sins like irreverence and impiety, wrath and murder, unchastity and adultery, covetousness and theft, as well as detraction and false speech, break down life's communal bonds with others because they prevent *communication*, the sharing of goods that we need from others and that others need from us.[6] These communal bonds are not only social but also physical: bearing burdens, being with one another in sorrow and celebra-

---

4. Radner, *A Time to Keep*, 92–96.

5. Radner, *A Time to Keep*, 110–11.

6. Augustine's *City of God*, bk. 19, continues to be a rich source of reflection on how created goods and our love for them should bind people together in justice and peace. See especially Oliver O'Donovan, *Common Objects of Love: Moral Reflection and the Shaping of Community* (Eerdmans, 2002). Somewhat differently, see Robert W. Jenson, "Politics and Sex," in *Systematic Theology*, vol. 2, *The Works of God* (Oxford University Press, 2001), 73–94.

tion, sharing physical touch (Matt. 27:24–61; Mark 5:21–43; John 11:17–37). This all belongs to the whole reality that God speaks with his Word and shapes by his Spirit when he creates any creature: the temporal and spatial contours of created life as it comes from others, lives with others, and is given for others who will come after it.

Second, our created lives also come from God through and with nonhuman creatures. This is already pronounced where we read that God "formed the man of dust from the ground" (Gen. 2:7). The association of human life with the ground is given in the association of the name Adam (*adam*) with "from the ground" (*adamah*). The fruitfulness and health of human life are therefore dependent, materially, on the fruitfulness and health of the soil.[7] Adam and Eve are given food from trees, which grow in soil (Gen. 2:16). Adam's dependence on the soil for his bread is cursed with frustration.

> In pain shall you eat of it all the days of your life;
> thorns and thistles it shall bring forth for you;
> and you shall eat the plants of the field.
> (Gen. 3:17–18)

Finally, just as Adam comes from the ground, he will eventually return to it.

> You are dust,
> and to dust you shall return. (Gen. 3:19)

7. See here Norman Wirzba, *This Sacred Life: Humanity's Place in a Wounded World* (Cambridge University Press, 2021), 63–122, who describes the mutual dependencies of created life as a "network" or "meshwork," richly illustrated with phenomenological, anthropological, and agrarian insights. These insights could be strengthened by more direct appeal to (1) divine action, especially the notion of God's mediate providence, which describes the textured way God provides for and works within created life, and (2) providence's deep background in God's wisdom and glory. Appeals like this would balance Wirzba's use of the term *animism*, which invites misunderstanding, despite being carefully deployed.

Thus, as agrarian writers like Wendell Berry helpfully remind us, human life is lived not so much "upon" as "from" the land.[8] We are dependent on it not only for what we eat but also for what we are. As Norman Wirzba explains, soil is "an indescribably complex intertwining of microbial communities that in their interactions with minerals, water, organic matter, and air produce the conditions for terrestrial life."[9] Our human lives are entangled with the lives of countless other organisms and life cycles all around us. As is evident in many nature documentaries and natural history museums, contemporary culture overemphasizes this truth and neglects or denies altogether the distinctiveness of human life. A similar temptation can beset theological reflection on the world and animal life. But such errors must not diminish the importance of how God gives created life through and with other created life.

The opportunity to sing is a shared privilege. Grasping this helps guard our own opportunity from potential threats. On the one hand, the connectedness of all created life gives the church reason to take seriously potential threats to other creatures, especially other humans, but also fish and water, birds and air, beasts and forests, bees and soil. All creatures depend on one another in myriad ways, many of which we do not even perceive. Humanity's reliance on other life forms and systems should fill us with awe and the fear of God, aware of how little we know and how much we need. On the other hand, the mutual dependence of other creatures reminds us that we are created to live *with* and not apart from other creatures, like the land and its inhabitants. Life disconnected from

8. Wendell Berry, "A Native Hill," in *The Art of the Commonplace: The Agrarian Essays of Wendell Berry*, ed. Norman Wirzba (Counterpoint, 2002), 7, cited by Wirzba, *This Sacred Life*, 70.

9. Wirzba, *This Sacred Life*, 72.

these realities—as so much modern life is—will inevitably run against the grain of what we are. No wonder, then, if life lived through digital technology leaves us feeling aimless, sorrowful, and anxious. Whatever disconnects us from reality forges a demonic counterfeit of life. God created us as real things meant to live alongside and draw support from other real things—other people especially, but also the goods of his creation. These are some of the ways we share the doxological opportunity of created life with all creation.

Creation's Common Doxology

Just as the opportunity to sing is shared, so is the singing itself. Creatures share a common opportunity to sing a common doxology, manifesting God's glory. Creatures glorify God through their fruitfulness because that is how they become semitransparent to God's life of fruitful love. Fruitfulness sounds like God's musicality. Hence, Jesus teaches us that spiritual fruitfulness glorifies God: "By this my Father is glorified, that you bear much fruit and so prove to be my disciples" (John 15:8; cf. Ps. 1:3; Matt. 5:16). The "fruit of the Spirit" defines those who belong to Jesus and who will inherit the kingdom of God with him (Gal. 5:22–24). All creation echoes this spiritual truth in the physical realm. Fruitfulness is how God blesses creatures. "Blessed shall be the fruit of your womb and the fruit of your ground and the fruit of your cattle, the increase of your herds and the young of your flock" (Deut. 28:4; cf. Ps. 128). God also glorifies himself in judgment by taking away fruitfulness and reminding us that he is its source, for God alone "gives the growth" (Isa. 32:9–20; Ezek. 19:10–14; 1 Cor. 3:7). God's glory fills the whole earth as he makes his people like a vineyard whose fruit fills the land (Isa. 6:3; 27:6; Hos. 14:4–8). Fruitfulness glorifies God. Indeed, Isaiah prophecies that God will display his glory in the wilderness when he causes it to

> blossom abundantly
> and rejoice with joy and singing. (Isa. 35:2)

The common doxology of creation is therefore how all things glorify God together by witnessing to God's fruitfulness with their own fruitfulness. They all do this together as they support and fulfill God's command to "be fruitful."[10]

Many creatures are capable of being fertile in their own ways. Generally, created life is fruitful as it passes on life to others in love and service. Humans do this in their own genealogies and relationships, bearing fruit physically as well as spiritually. Our Lord does this in his own genealogy within the church, bearing fruit through the branches connected to him (John 15:4–5). God gives life—even his own—to make life fruitful. And so on for plant and animal life. Even though angels are not reproductively fruitful (Matt. 22:30), they nevertheless cultivate the fruitfulness of the kingdom of God (Ps. 103:21; Heb. 1:7). This alerts us to the fact that while all creatures sing a common doxology, they are not fruitful equally or in the same ways. Some are less fruitful than others; some differently fruitful. Angels are fruitful differently from plants and humans. "Star differs from star in glory" (1 Cor. 15:41). And there may be many reasons why: not merely differences of nature and capacity but different conditions those natures enjoy and inequalities of opportunity (illness, disability, and so forth). What counts is that creatures bear fruit in senses appropriate to their natures and their roles within the whole created order.

Creatures who are incapable of being fruitful themselves nevertheless support and nurture the fruitfulness of other creatures.

10. Gen. 1:22, 28; 8:17; 9:1, 7; 28:3.

In this section we considered "living creatures"; I've said almost nothing about inanimate creatures. Yet even these creatures serve the fruitfulness of the whole in their own roles. For example, the moon serves fruitfulness as it does what it was created to do: not only in preserving the earth's climate and tide cycles, without which much else could not be fruitful, but also in governing the passage of days within creation's doxological rhythm.

Creatures glorify God in concert as a created order by being fruitful and supporting the fruitfulness of the whole created order. This is a large part of creation's overall harmony, its musical answer to the Creator. Creation's common doxology comes from its common orientation to God's glory. And all things yearn for God's glory much as flowers incline toward the sun, blossoming as they reach up to it. In this way, everything testifies to its source in God's life of fruitful love.

The Orchestra: Its Organization Under Humanity

We have just explored how created life is a shared opportunity to sing a shared doxology. This took us into the truth of the mutual dependencies of creatures, the sense in which they are a sort of community. We began to stumble upon the important differences found within these mutual dependencies. Creatures are connected by what they have in common, certainly, but also by their differences from one another. When we keep both the commonalities and differences of creatures in view, we may appreciate how creatures together constitute a grand symphony orchestra of the Creator's praise.

With the metaphor of an "orchestra," we are concerned with how creation's order includes differences between creatures that hint at a limited but real hierarchy.[11] Organization and even a

---

11. The discussion here builds on the previous discussions of creation's order in terms of creation's end (see chap. 2, under "Why God Opens His Musicality," p. 52) as

degree of hierarchy are essential to the proper functioning of a symphony orchestra. An orchestra is incomplete without its four families of instruments (strings, woodwinds, brass, and percussion) as well as its instrumentalists. Moreover, these all occupy the stage in a certain order; the more blaring instruments are located at the back, so they don't drown out the strings up front. And at the head of the orchestra is the conductor, who governs the whole by interpreting the music, setting the rhythm, and providing cues for the various parts to work together. Something analogous is true of the orchestra of creatures, conducted by the human liturgist. Just like the families of instruments, creatures are differentiated from one another such that they sound out different tones. And similar to the role of the conductor, humans stand at the top of the created hierarchy because they are appointed to lead the cosmic liturgy. We may understand the differences and hierarchy between creatures in terms of (1) the different *kinds* of creatures and (2) their different *ends*.[12]

Different Kinds of Creatures

The first difference between creatures Scripture mentions is that God created plants, trees, sea creatures, birds, other varieties of animals, and insects "according to their kinds" (Gen. 1:11–12, 21, 24–25). This difference belongs to the distinctions the Creator draws between things, distinctions that ultimately provide the conditions for their fruitfulness (Gen. 1:12, 22; 8:17). Part of creation's order is therefore the order of different *kinds* of creatures. Beasts are not birds are not plants are not insects, and so on. Creation's rich diversity is not the deceptive appear-

---

well as its wholeness (see chap. 4, under "Hearing What God's Creative Word Speaks," p. 85).

12. This discussion of kinds and ends, generic and teleological order, is inspired by Oliver O'Donovan, *Resurrection and Moral Order: An Outline for Evangelical Ethics*, 2nd ed. (Eerdmans, 1994), 31–52. As O'Donovan notes, everyone makes judgments about creation's order; it inevitably informs all moral and political philosophy.

ance amid a more fundamental identity of creatures with one another. Rather, each created kind is a distinct witness to God's goodness, some more brilliant than others (1 Cor. 15:39–41). The differentiation of kinds means that humans, for all their similarities with other land creatures, are distinct from them. Humans, land animals, and sea creatures are all "living creatures" (Gen. 1:20; 2:7, 19). Humans and land animals both come from the ground and return to it (Gen. 1:24; 2:7; Eccl. 3:20), as does plant life (Gen. 1:11). But humans are not mere creatures alongside others. One evidence of this is that unlike mere animal and vegetable life, for instance, humans are not made according to "kinds" (Gen. 1:27). They are unique.

There is one kind of human, made from one and the same soil (Acts 17:26). The ideology of "blood and soil," which says there are different kinds of humans with different moral and cultural capacities according to which some are more "worthy" than others (of life, political supremacy, etc.), is fundamentally pagan.[13] Scripture of course acknowledges the differences between human cultures, ethnicities, and nations. But it refuses to consider these grounds for subordinating some humans to others, or for segregating them in family, public, and church life.[14] All humans are, rather, made in God's "own image"

13. Cf. Joseph Ratzinger, *The Divine Project: Reflections on Creation and the Church* (Ignatius, 2023), 68. For an illuminating discussion of one such pagan ideology in antiquity and the early Christian response, see Matthew R. Crawford, "The Emperor Julian and Cyril of Alexandria on Human Nature, Ethnicity, and Moral Progress," *Ephemerides Theologicae Lovanienses* 100, no. 1 (2024): 73–102. In this connection, one should also remember Karl Barth's critique of national identity in *Church Dogmatics*, 3/4, ed. G. W. Bromiley and T. F. Torrance, trans. A. T. Mackay et al. (T&T Clark, 1961), 298–323.

14. Old Testament prohibitions against marrying pagans have nothing to do with some mythology of created ethnic hierarchies (pagans had such mythologies) and everything to do with faithfulness to God. Even Jesus's Jewish genealogy, therefore, includes faithful Canaanites and a Moabite (Matt. 1:3–5). The reason Israelites were to separate from pagans was to avoid the threat of idolatry (Ex. 34:13–16; Deut. 7:3–4; Josh. 23:12–13; Ezra 9:1–2; cf. Amos 1:3–2:3), starkly illustrated in the paradoxical foolishness of the eminently wise Solomon (1 Kings 11:1–2). In this respect, Paul echoes these prohibitions in the New Testament concerning new marriages and friendships (1 Cor. 5:9–11; 2 Cor. 6:14–18; cf. Lev. 19:19) while making allowances within existing

(Gen. 1:27). Hence, though we may and should classify creatures according to kinds, we may not classify humans according to kinds. Here we have only one kind: God's image bearer, whose flesh God graced in our Lord's incarnation.

Creation's orchestra includes different kinds of creatures and therefore different families of instruments with a variety of sounds, notes, and beats. Like the different languages that all praise the Creator at Pentecost, the many voices of creatures glorify him more together than apart. Indeed, part of humanity's priestly role in leading the cosmic liturgy is to bring together the different voices of creation into the voice of the church's liturgy. Creatures are meant to make music together, with the human uniquely serving as their conductor. To see this, we must consider the different ends belonging to these families.

Different Ends of Creatures

The order of the orchestra includes not only different families of instruments but also different *ends*—they all have different roles and produce different sounds. In our discussion of creation's end, we distinguished between intrinsic and extrinsic ends.[15] The intrinsic ends of creatures describe how they naturally flourish within the created order, in relation to themselves and to others. This is how they glorify God by their mere existence. Within these intrinsic ends, including the mutual dependencies of creatures mentioned above, some creatures nevertheless are ordered in relation to others in ways that are unequal and asymmetrical.

Creation's order means that some creatures support and serve the fruitfulness of others without mutually receiving the

marriages (1 Cor. 7:12–16; cf. Rom. 11:16; Acts 16:1). None of this signals a retreat from the world, but the church's consecration *within* it (John 17:14–19).

15. See chap. 2, under "Why God Opens His Musicality" (p. 52).

same support. And ends help us understand this order. Animals and birds are not ordered in relation to streams in the same way that streams are to them.

> They give drink to every beast of the field;
> the wild donkeys quench their thirst.
> Beside them the birds of the heavens dwell;
> they sing among the branches. (Ps. 104:11–12)

Neither are animals and humans subservient to grass and plants, despite their dependence on the land for their fruitfulness.

> You cause the grass to grow for the livestock
> and plants for man to cultivate,
> that he may bring forth food from the earth
> and wine to gladden the heart of man,
> oil to make his face shine
> and bread to strengthen man's heart. (Ps. 104:14–15)

Scripture spells out many such relations: trees serve birds, mountains and hills support goats and rock badgers (Ps. 104:16–18). All such relationships are representative and limited: representative because animals who benefit from the mountains include more than just goats and rock badgers, for instance; and limited because created things like trees have ends that stretch far beyond providing shelter to birds. Nevertheless, there is order between the different kinds of ends creatures have.

As we consider the order of these different ends, humans occupy a central place within creation—one with unique responsibilities and privileges. Although humans should tend the land, cultivate plant life, and care for the life of their beasts, this is not because humans are subordinate to these other creatures. Rather, land, plants, and beasts have been given to humanity and entrusted to their care (Gen. 1:29; 9:2–3; Ps. 115:16).[16] These things are under humanity in an important sense. They even give their lives to sustain ours. Humans depend on these other creatures without being subject to them. Hence, there is a certain inequality between humans and animals, even in the sight of God. "Look at the birds of the air: they neither sow nor reap nor gather into barns, and yet your heavenly Father feeds them. Are you not of more value than they?" (Matt. 6:26; cf. 10:29–31; 12:11–12).

The sequence of days within the creation hymn also suggests the order between creatures and the unique place of humans. Herman Bavinck observes that the days of creation "contain a suggestion of the relationship of rank in which these creatures stand over against each other." He continues:

> No scientific investigation can overthrow this relationship. The formless precedes the formed in rank and order, the inorganic precedes the organic, the plant precedes the animal, and the animal precedes man. Man is and remains the crown of creation: the making and the preparation of the earth issues in him, and converges upon him. . . . In a religious and moral sense [the earth] remains the center of the universe. . . . It has been chosen to be the arena of struggle in which the great battle must be fought against every evil power. It has been chosen to serve as the place for the establishment of the kingdom of heaven.[17]

This is almost right. Creation's sixth day is the climactic moment of God's creative work, and it culminates in the making of man and woman, who are the primary respondents in

16. Thoughtful care for animals belongs to the character God's law seeks to cultivate. John Kessler, *Old Testament Theology: Divine Call and Human Response* (Baylor University Press, 2013), 157–60.

17. Herman Bavinck, *Our Reasonable Faith*, trans. Henry Zylstra (Eerdmans, 1956), 173. C. S. Lewis's "space trilogy" illustrates this point feverishly.

the liturgy. Hence their royal and priestly "dominion" over creation (Gen. 1:26). But the real crown of creation is featured on the seventh day: God's rest.[18] The diverse kinds of creatures and their different ends serve the glory of God. Nevertheless, humans do this in a way surpassing all other creatures through their intentional, conscious praise, which gathers other forms of created praise within its reach. In this regard, the similarities between creation and the temple highlight the priestly role of humanity within creation's order.[19] Creatures are the orchestra of this cosmic symphony, and humans are its conductors, liturgists of creation's music. As goes the conductor, so goes the orchestra.

Human Disorder and the Vanity of Creation

Thus far we have seen that creatures are a symphony orchestra who all share the same musical opportunity within a particular organization under humanity, who serves as its conductor. However, this orchestra is frustrated, unable to achieve the grand harmonies for which it was created. Glimpses of music break through, but amid disorder and failure. Creation is subject to "futility" or vanity (Rom. 8:20). A responsible doctrine of creation must square with these facts, because they baffle us: We are a mist that vanishes as quickly as it appears (James 4:14). Life and the pursuit of the joy for which we are made seems vaporous and out of reach. "All is vanity" (Eccl. 1:2). Why is this so?

Humans are meant to live within God's good creation in such a way that promotes its fruitfulness, unto the glory of God. Doxologically, this means that they do such mundane things as

18. L. Michael Morales, *Who Shall Ascend the Mountain of the Lord? A Biblical Theology of the Book of Leviticus*, NSBT 37 (IVP Academic, 2015), 43–49.

19. On these similarities, see chap. 1, under "From Cosmos to Temple" (p. 24).

farming and trading, eating and wearing clothes, organizing common life and preserving justice, with God's Sabbath rest on the horizon. Creation is meant to benefit from this rest along with humanity, as we see in laws about giving the land and beasts "rest" (Lev. 25:1–7; Deut. 5:14). As humans live within creation's doxological rhythm and abide by its distinctions and order, they receive all that has been entrusted to their dominion with fear and gratitude before God. Originally, this should have resulted in harmony and the expansion of Eden's consecrated time and space to cover the four corners of the earth. Creation would have followed humanity's lead much like the eschatological vision of the nations flocking to Zion so God may rule over them (Isa. 2:2–4).[20] But this did not happen, as Adam and Eve got it into their heads that they could lead the liturgy on their own terms, apart from God's word (cf. Lev. 10:1–2). Soon after its assembly, creation's orchestra was led by conductors drunk on their own pride.

Creation consequently suffered much as an orchestra would: Its rhythm ignored, its order subverted, creation fell into dissonance and disorder. Only a few generations from Adam, "all flesh had corrupted their way on the earth" (Gen. 6:12). Scripture is not specific, but somehow this corruption extends from humanity to all creation. Here it's important to remember that sin and disorder are distinct. All sin is disorder, but not all disorder is sin. So, while only humans and angels sin, their disorder infects the rest of the creation with disorder.[21] Furthermore, creation suffers from God's curse. This begins with the

20. John Goldingay, *Old Testament Theology*, vol. 3, *Israel's Life* (IVP Academic, 2009), 624.

21. Scripture explicitly teaches that angels sinned (John 8:44; 2 Pet. 2:4). The angelic fall preceded the human fall, not least because it was a fallen angel, Satan, who tempted Adam and Eve in the garden (Gen. 3:1; Rev. 12:9). Augustine, *City of God* 12.1–9, develops a theologically rich account of the angelic fall that nevertheless needs surer footing exegetically.

cursing of the serpent, who will now be at "enmity" with humans (Gen. 3:15), a sign of how wild beasts will similarly pose threats (Lev. 26:6). The disorder continues with the cursing of the woman's fruitfulness, her childbearing now threatened with toilsome danger (Gen. 3:16). And the disorder concludes with cursing the land itself, the fruitfulness of which will now require significant toil (Gen. 3:17). Creation is therefore not so much a "fallen world" as disordered and cursed, reflecting humans' disorder back to them.

The prophets often speak of creation "mourning" this disorder it suffers.[22] For instance, God brings a lawsuit against Israel, whose sentence falls upon creatures within humanity's dominion:

> Hear the word of the Lord, O children of Israel,
> for the Lord has a controversy with the inhabitants of the land.
> There is no faithfulness or steadfast love,
> and no knowledge of God in the land;
> there is swearing, lying, murder, stealing, and committing adultery;
> they break all bounds, and bloodshed follows bloodshed.
> Therefore the land mourns,
> and all who dwell in it languish,
> and also the beasts of the field
> and the birds of the heavens,
> and even the fish of the sea are taken away. (Hos. 4:1–3)

The communal bonds governed by the second table of the law are broken, and so too is the created order's harmony. The

22. Richard Bauckham, *The Bible and Ecology: Rediscovering the Community of Creation* (Baylor University Press, 2010), 92–102. See also Isa. 24:4; 33:9; Jer. 4:23–28; 9:12–14; 12:4; 23:10; Joel 1:10; Amos 1:2.

disorder of humans and the disorder of creation are intertwined, as is their order.[23] When the Lord blesses his people with peace, the created order benefits as well (Ezek. 34:25–31; Zech. 8:12–13). And when the Lord curses his people, the creation is cursed with them.

Hence, Paul links the future hope of God's adopted sons with creation's mourning and longing.

> Creation waits with eager longing for the revealing of the sons of God. For the creation was subjected to futility, not willingly, but because of him who subjected it, in hope that the creation itself will be set free from its bondage to corruption and obtain the freedom of the glory of the children of God. (Rom. 8:19–21)[24]

Creation's "futility" is its inability to sing as it ought, to achieve its intrinsic and extrinsic ends. God subjected creation to this futility—no one else could—because and as humanity itself "became futile in their thinking" (Rom. 1:21; cf. Eph. 4:17–18). At the heart of this futility is turning away from God's Word and submitting to idolatry (Acts 14:15). Futility takes over human life and the world as humanity becomes centered on the world rather than on God, listening to other

23. It may sound odd to associate creation's disorder with human disorder, but it's rather intuitive upon further consideration. We need only think about how human actions impact animals to see that this makes good sense. Abused animals, such as dogs, display in their dispositions and actions the effects of mistreatment. Similar rippling effects of greed and foolishness branch out onto forests, soil, and oceans through excessive deforestation, overcultivation, and overfishing. Human corruption corrupts. And who can draw the line where this corruption stops? Bavinck is correct to observe how sin forms a sort of parasitic "organism" that infects the whole world it enters (*Our Reasonable Faith*, 246–49). Since the good of one creature is linked together with the good of others, the privation of one's goodness affects others. Sins are linked together (cf. James 2:10), and so are their consequences ("to the third and fourth generations"). Our transgressions never happen in a bubble, isolated from the world around us. Rather, they splinter in thousands of directions and slip from view, infecting more than we can know.

24. See here Thomas R. Schreiner, *Romans*, Baker Exegetical Commentary on the New Testament, 2nd ed. (Baker Academic, 2018), 423–33; Trevor J. Burke, *Adopted into God's Family: Exploring a Pauline Metaphor*, NSBT 22 (IVP Academic, 2006), 177–93.

words and being led by other spirits, not the Spirit who gives us the Word (1 John 4:1–6). Creation's subjection to futility is therefore the frustration of its intended harmony with the Word, with the result that chaos threatens the created order. Since creation's fruitfulness is frustrated by the threats of toil, so is its doxology.

Creation is therefore not the way it should be. Nonhuman creatures are not fit to be liturgists. By abandoning their liturgical responsibilities, humanity follows rather than leads the orchestra. Humans have become like beasts in their foolishness and lack of wisdom (Job 35:11; Ps. 32:9; Prov. 26:3). They try to blend in with the rest of creation rather than stand out (Gen. 3:8), so they imitate beasts by pursuing sex, food, and other created goods with mere animal appetites.[25] Hence, "the world" divorced from its liturgical harmony is full of "the desires of the flesh and the desires of the eyes and pride of life" (1 John 2:16).

The resultant disorder has left all things longing for human priests to lead its liturgy and restore its harmony with the Word. This can only happen with the "revealing of the sons of God" in their resurrection, who inherit God himself and the whole creation with Christ, thereby entering glory (Rom. 8:19). In their resurrection, God's people will be conformed to the true and faithful Son (Rom. 8:29), for then their lowly bodies will be like his "glorious body" (Phil. 3:21). When the Word conforms his people to himself, the glory within them will redound to the creation, which will be liberated from sin's corruption.

25. Augustine, *The Literal Meaning of Genesis* 11.32.43, argues that humanity became like the animals in death and sensuousness (*WSA* I/13:453). Hildegard of Bingen, *Scivias*, trans. Columba Hart and Jane Bishop, Classics of Western Spirituality (Paulist Press, 1990), 1.2.15 (81), argues similarly that fornication is beast-like. Yet, even here we must recognize how human disorder is actually *worse* than beastly. Humans use their greater resources of intellect and industry to become ever more harmful and perverse to one another and the rest of creation. Humanity is ordered to a higher end than beasts are, and it therefore corrupts more deeply.

God has subjected creation "in this hope" because God intends something more for his "sons," and therefore something more for their inheritance—namely, glory (Rom. 8:18, 24).

Conclusion

The shared opportunity to sing is fulfilled together or not at all, and it must be fulfilled by "the son of man" who has been given "dominion" over God's creation (Ps. 8:4–6). So important is the role of God's image bearers in the created order that the orchestra of creatures succeeds or fails with them. We failed when we stole the forbidden fruit (Gen. 3:2–3). And the result was that we bore the rotten fruit of self-glorification. Our fruitfulness became subject to futility. Hence, subsequent to the fall, human futility has branched out and sown dissonance in our relations to all things. At its core, this futility resides in spurning God's Word and Spirit for demonic words and spirits, and therefore demonic conceptions of the order of God's created "words" (cf. Lam. 2:14; Ezek. 13:1–8; Rom. 1:21; Eph. 4:17). The present dissonance and vexation that plagues God's creation testifies to its need for the Word, through whom alone it is made whole, and whose sacrifice liberates us from "the futile ways inherited from [our] forefathers" (1 Pet. 1:18). And thus we have good reason to pray, "Come, Lord Jesus" (Rev. 22:20). Praying this, we ask the one through whom all things have been made to make all things new (Rev. 21:5). Having turned away from the Word, we need to be turned back to him. We need conversion to the Word, the hope of all creation.[26] The song needs a resolution.

26. Athanasius, *On the Incarnation* 8 (PPS 44a:67), therefore uses metaphors of *turning* or *conversion* (*epistrophē*) to describe how the Word rescues creatures from corruption. See also Augustine, *The Literal Meaning of Genesis* 1.4.9; Maximus, *Ambiguum* 7.20; and O'Donovan, *Resurrection and Moral Order*, 91–94.

6

The Song's Resolution

Creation's Fulfillment in Christ

In the wake of creation's devastation by human sin, the Creator's song is full of tensions that run through us all. There are digressions that seem to go nowhere and whose purposes we misunderstand and even doubt. Having turned away from God's Word, all of us have desires in tension with the fulfillments this world offers and live in tension with the death that has reigned since Adam. Believers have faith in God's promises and providence that is in tension with the devastation we see, and more. Creation's harmony is difficult to hear and feel unless we are attuned to God's Word.

Jesus Christ resolves these tensions and makes sense of the song's various digressions, for he is the song's melody, "the Alpha and the Omega, the first and the last, the beginning and the end" (Rev. 22:13). All things were not only created through Jesus Christ, after all, but also created for him (Col. 1:16). In the incarnate Word himself, we can hear what the song is and where it's going. Jesus resolves the Creator's song by fulfilling its liturgy. He is the orchestra's chief conductor, the great high priest of the new covenant, who frees creation from futility, for worship. Everything we've seen in previous chapters concerning God's creative end, his generosity, his distinguishing and forming, as well as his harmonizing of the song's notes and subjecting its orchestra to frustration, all comes to a head in Christ.

To this end, we must examine three things: (1) how Christ summarizes all the song in his own sonship, revealing creation as an inheritance; (2) how Christ receives this inheritance by fulfilling creation's liturgy; and, finally, (3) how Christ leads creation to God's Sabbath rest.

Song and Sonship: Creation as Our Lost Inheritance

The song's arrangement, or what the biblical authors simply call the "economy" (1 Tim. 1:4), comes together in Jesus.[1] Economies aim at goals, and they organize things to achieve these goals. Creation's economy is God's orderly arrangement of all things that aims at his intended goal or end for all things. God's economy therefore embodies God's plan, "the mystery of his will" (Eph. 1:9). And this mystery centers on Jesus, the song's melody. Everything Jesus is, including his life, death, and resurrection, is the most memorable part of the song. Mysteriously, even grains falling to the earth, dying, and bearing fruit belong to this melody (John 12:24). In this section, we must see (1) how Jesus discloses God's ultimate purpose for creation, which is (2) to be an inheritance of God's sons.

1. The Greek word behind the English term *economy* (*oikonomia*) is typically translated as "plan" (Eph. 1:10; 3:9) or "stewardship" (1 Cor. 9:17).

Bringing It All Together

Jesus reveals God's plan for creation in the "fullness of time" with his incarnation, and its goal is "to unite all things in Christ, things in heaven and things on earth" (Eph. 1:10; cf. Gal. 4:4). Paul's word for this process of "uniting" or gathering together all things in Christ, sometimes called "recapitulation," means "bringing something to a head" (*anakephalaiōsis*). We might think of this as a summary that includes things while it concludes them. This process ties together what it brings together by putting a "cap" on it all. In this sense, Jesus summarizes God's mysterious purposes in creation much as the commands to love God and neighbor summarize both tables of the law (Mark 12:28–31).[2]

The way Jesus brings all things to a head in himself is unexpected and new, weaving in counterpoints, but it also fits what precedes it. Christ restates and brings together creation's original purpose, its rhythm and order, as well as its failures, the many digressions the song takes and their resulting tensions. We see this especially in how Jesus "relives" the lives of key figures like Adam and Israel, but with reversals and new themes incorporated. In this respect, Jesus summarizes all our lives within himself. For whenever we read of people like Adam or of nations like Israel, Scripture speaks to us as Nathan did to David: "You are the man!" (2 Sam. 12:7).[3] Our lives are narrated for us in the lives of these sinners and saints. But to find out where these lives lead, we must look to Jesus. He is the Word in whom all these lives hold together as parts of a coherent song. Since

2. Paul says that the command to love one's neighbor "recapitulates" the second table of the law, about honoring those in authority, not murdering, not coveting, and so forth (Rom. 13:9). By the same logic, the command to love God (Deut. 6:5) recapitulates the first table of the law, concerned with exclusive worship of God and avoiding idolatry (cf. Matt. 22:37–40).

3. Further, see Oswald Bayer, *A Contemporary in Dissent: Johann Georg Hamann as a Radical Enlightener*, trans. Roy A. Harrisville and Mark C. Mattes (Eerdmans, 2012), 46–62.

he brings them to a head in himself, Scripture also speaks to us as Pilate did to the chief priests: "Behold the man!" (John 19:5). That is, behold the Word, who alone defines us and the meaning of our lives. Behold the Word, who defines all things.

Jesus is therefore a "reprise" of the Creator's song: All its rhythm and order are included in the melody's reappearance in a new key as the song moves toward its resolution. Yet the song's reprise is also a surprise.[4] The church looms large in this reprise. Jesus fulfills God's purposes for creation through his purposes for his people. The visible sign of these purposes is the church, particularly its unity and worship. For here, just as he does in creation, Jesus gathers differences for the sake of fruitfulness. Christ is the head of a body (Eph. 1:22–23) in which "wills that were before in conflict are made to harmonize."[5] Though "many" members, they are all are "one body in Christ" (Rom. 12:5; Eph. 4:4). He draws together Jew and Gentile (Gal. 3:28), who had been separated by the covenants of promise, so that they may all be "members of the household of God" (Eph. 2:11–19). He brings together male and female, circumcised and uncircumcised, slave and free—people separated by creation, ritual observance, or socioeconomic status—so that they are all "one in Christ" and therefore "Abraham's offspring, heirs according to promise" (Gal. 3:28–29; cf. Gen. 3:16). He also brings together "things in heaven and things on earth"—all the earth represented by sinful humanity and all the heavenly realm represented by God—so that they may now harmonize with God and one another (Eph. 1:10; Col. 1:20). Jesus reconciles the world to himself so that all things can be reconciled with one another in him (2 Cor. 5:19). As the church is "filled with the Spirit," its members address one another "in psalms

4. Michel Bouttier, *L'Épître de saint Paul aux Éphésiens* (Labor et Fides, 1991), 70, 296.
5. Aquinas, *Commentary on Colossians* 1.5.53.

and hymns and spiritual songs, singing and making melody to the Lord" (Eph. 5:19). As the Spirit brings them the Word, creation's melody, the church makes its own melody. It is doxologically fruitful. The world's harmony cannot make sense apart from Jesus, but "in him all things hold together" (Col. 1:17).

The "recapitulation" of all things in Christ is the outworking of God's covenant promises. Jesus resolves the movements and tensions in the lives of God's people, such as Adam, Abraham, and David—movements and tensions that are ours. Therefore, it is revealing when we read that God the Father appointed his Son "the heir of all things, through whom he also created the world" (Heb. 1:2).[6] Song and sonship belong together in Christ. All things were thus created "for" Christ, who is their heir (Rom. 8:17; Col. 1:16). He is the "son of man" who has dominion over all things, who was made "for a little while . . . lower than the angels" but is now "crowned with glory and honor" (Heb. 2:9; cf. Ps. 8:4–6; Dan. 7:14). Christ uses our humanity as his instrument to show us our part in the Creator's song.[7] God always intended for creation to be an inheritance received by his "sons" as they lead its song of praise, so that all things might rest in harmony with the Creator. The inheritance comes to us through liturgy because it is a doxological song of God's glory.

Creation as Inheritance

Throughout Scripture, God pursues his creative purpose of raising sons to receive creation as their inheritance.[8] Their call to

6. Note how themes of inheritance and sonship sit alongside creation in John's prologue (John 1:3, 12–13), or how adoption as sons and inheritance are connected to creation's longing and hope by Paul (Rom. 8:15–21).

7. Cf. Cyril of Alexandria, *Scholia on the Incarnation of the Only Begotten* 25, in John McGuckin, *St. Cyril of Alexandria: The Christological Controversy, Its History, Theology, and Texts* (Brill, 1994), 320.

8. The exegetical reflections in this chapter have been sharpened especially by Trevor J. Burke, *Adopted into God's Family: Exploring a Pauline Metaphor*, NSBT 22 (IVP Academic, 2006); Scott W. Hahn, *Kinship by Covenant: A Canonical Approach*

sonship comes with doxological responsibilities, leading creation to its appointed end in God's rest. This requires that they receive and minister God's word. Adam was the first "son of God" (Luke 3:38), commissioned with royal and priestly duties to govern God's household in accordance with God's word until he would inherit it (Gen. 1:28; 2:15). Similarly, Israel was God's "firstborn son" (Ex. 4:22–23), who was called to be "a royal priesthood" and light among the nations in the land they would inherit (Ex. 19:6; Deut. 4:21). Adam would inherit God's seventh-day rest (Gen. 2:2–3), and Israel would inherit the "rest" of the promised land.[9] Just as God's rest crowned creation, so rest crowns the inheritance; they belong together (Deut. 12:9).

Before they receive these inheritances and crowns, God's children first have to grow into "mature manhood" (Eph. 4:13; cf. Luke 2:52). Growth always precedes fruitfulness; God inscribed this law into the very fabric of created life. Adam's life was always going to be a pathway, a pilgrimage through time marked by the dignity of work, struggle, and wisdom. Sin merely frustrated these goods and made them toilsome. But life was never meant to be a vacation in paradise, some perpetual stagnation. Life was meant to be lived. Human life is an apprenticeship within the Father's household, in this sense. It is a proving ground for those who would inherit the earth.

Adam's growth would have borne fruit in keeping with the song's melody had he submitted to the Word, ordering all things to the rest found in harmony with the Creator (Matt. 3:8; John 15:4). The same calling came to Israel: "You shall not turn aside to the right hand or to the left. You shall walk in all the

---

to the Fulfillment of God's Saving Promises (Yale University Press, 2009), 278–327; Perl Jarle Bekken, *Paul's Negotiation of Abraham in Galatians 3 in the Jewish Context: The Galatian Converts—Lineal Descendants of Abraham and Heirs of the Promise* (De Gruyter, 2021), 247–78.

9. Ex. 3:8; Num. 34:2; Josh. 11:22; 22:2–4.

way that the LORD your God has commanded you, that you may live, and that it may go well with you, and that you may live long in the land that you shall possess" (Deut. 5:32–33; cf. Josh. 1:8). To foster this growth, Adam was meant to trust the "Father of lights" as the source of "every good gift and every perfect gift" (James 1:17). He was to wait for his inheritance patiently (Heb. 6:15). If he had done so, he would have known ever more deeply his Father's generous heart.

> What father among you, if his son asks for a fish, will instead of a fish give him a serpent; or if he asks for an egg, will give him a scorpion? If you then, who are evil, know how to give good gifts to your children, how much more will the heavenly Father give the Holy Spirit to those who ask him! (Luke 11:11–13)

However, these sons of God rebelled and forfeited their Father's inheritance. Both Adam and Israel turned away from God and from their liturgical vocation to receive, heed, and minister God's word.[10] God consequently disinherited them with an oath:

> I swore in my wrath,
> "They shall not enter my rest." (Ps. 95:11)

The lives of Adam and Israel thereby became sorrowful themes in God's song. But Jesus subsumes these themes into a greater harmony.

Jesus gathers Adam's and Israel's temptations in his own wilderness, where Satan offers him "all the kingdoms of the world and their glory" (Matt. 4:8). Unlike Adam and Israel, however, the true Son lives by the words of his Father and not those of his enemies (Matt. 4:4; John 8:47). He waits for a greater inheritance and glory that cannot be seized but can only be received

10. Gen. 3:4–5; Ex. 32:1–6; cf. Josh. 24:14–15; Matt. 4:4.

as his Father's gift (Matt. 28:18; John 17:1–5). Jesus does this in fulfillment of God's promises to Abraham and David, which answer the rebellion of Adam and Israel, respectively.[11] Both of these promises are "oaths" that move in the direction of inheriting rather than disinheriting wayward sons. These oaths are early notes belonging to the Creator's "new song," which resolves the tensions of the original.

First, God swore an oath to Abraham that he would bless the nations through him, and that his "offspring" would receive the promised inheritance.[12] This inheritance began with the promise of land (Gen. 12:7). This answers Adam's failure to subdue the land, which would involve removing its threats and cultivating its fruitfulness (Gen. 1:26–28). God initially did this through Joshua, who led Abraham's offspring into the promised land, where they experienced "rest" from their enemies (Josh. 21:43–45). But both land and rest pointed beyond themselves to greater mysteries within God's promise. The land did not yet encompass "all the nations of the earth," prefiguring something global (Gen. 22:18; Ps. 2:8; Rom. 4:13). Israel's rest was temporary and had to be won in every new generation, prefiguring something permanent (2 Sam. 7:1; 1 Kings 5:4). Jesus (whose name is Greek for Joshua) gathers these notes within himself and finally leads his people to inherit both land (creation) and rest (eternal life).

Second, God also swore to David that his Son's throne would be established permanently when he would be appointed a

> priest forever
> after the order of Melchizedek. (Ps. 110:4)[13]

11. Gen. 15:7–8, 18–21; 17:15–21; 2 Sam. 7:2–27; 1 Chron. 17:3–15; Ps. 89:3–4, 27–29; Heb. 1:5–2:18.
12. Gen. 15:18; 22:16–18; Heb. 6:14–15; 11:8.
13. Cf. Gen. 14:17–24; 2 Sam. 7:8–16; Ps. 89:3–4; Heb. 1:5–14; 5:5–10; 6:20.

This shows how God fulfills the oath to Abraham's "offspring," who is also the Son of David (Rom. 1:3; Gal. 3:16). Melchizedek is a strange figure. He is both king and priest. He predates the law and the Levitical priesthood, occupying an "order" of priesthood all his own, which mediates God's promises rather than God's law. Jesus gathers these odd, early notes in himself and makes harmony: Melchizedek is "without father or mother or genealogy, having neither beginning of days nor end of life, but resembling the Son of God he continues a priest forever" (Heb. 7:3). Here is a greater King and Priest than any that came before, an "indestructible" one (Heb. 7:16). He can therefore bring Abraham's offspring to their permanent inheritance in its full scope (Heb. 8:6; 9:12). Jesus restores God's "sons" to their liturgical vocation and thereby makes them coheirs with him. God's promises provide both song and sonship by giving us his song in his Son.

As creation's melody, Jesus reveals and consummates the song's purposes as he resolves its tensions. The parable of the prodigal son is a portrait of this resolution. Within Adam, humanity is the prodigal son, who has seized his inheritance unseasonably and squandered it in a "far country," where he is as good as dead, envying swine (Luke 15:12–16). Reread in light of Christ, both sons in the parable have a different Head on their shoulders. In Jesus, the prodigal son, "came to himself" and returned to his Father's household, having been raised from the dead (Luke 15:17, 32) by one without sin (Luke 15:18; Heb. 2:16; 4:15). And in Jesus, the older son, who has "all" that belongs to his Father (Matt. 28:18; Luke 15:17, 31; John 16:15) is "not ashamed" of his brothers (Heb. 2:11). Instead of begrudging his brother's repentance, Jesus rejoices with the angelic servants of his Father's household over his prodigal sibling's return (Luke 15:7, 21). "Christ is faithful over God's house as a son" (Heb. 3:6), and it delights him to make us "fellow heirs" with him (Rom. 8:17). God reveals his creative purposes in Jesus, who receives and fulfills them as the faithful liturgist Adam should have been (Heb. 2:17; 8:2).

Receiving the Song: Inheritance and Liturgy

Bringing creation to a head, Jesus reveals and fulfills God's creative purposes. We have just seen how Jesus summarizes God's creative purposes in his "new song" that includes the original but transposes it into a different key. The melody that has held the song together will bring it to its resolution. He is therefore "appointed the heir of all things," as Adam should have been (Heb. 1:2). Hence, the song's final movement has appeared in "these last days" and is playing out before the world in the church (Heb. 1:2). We "do not yet see" the fulfillment of this final movement, but "we see him," the song's melody, and so we know the song's various notes and digressions will end in harmony (Heb. 2:8–9).

According to Hebrews, our confidence here is based on Jesus's shed blood, his perfect service on behalf of his people before God (Heb. 3:6; 4:16; 10:35). As Jesus resolves creation's tensions and fulfills God's creative purposes, he reveals creation as an inheritance received liturgically with sacrifice. In other words, God achieves his purpose for creation through the worship Jesus leads.

Receiving the Inheritance Through Liturgy

Liturgy is how we receive a creation that is doxological. We know this because creation is song, "doxology," a hymn of glory from the Creator that should sweep us up and return to him in praise. God glorifies himself in creation so that we may be glorified in him. But since we have sought our own glory, trying to improvise our way to immortality, the Word must reconcile us to himself and lead the doxology for us. Jesus thereby brings Adam's original liturgical responsibility to a head and carries it further up and further in than Adam could have imagined.

In the beginning, Adam was given a liturgical commission over creation. God "put him in the garden of Eden to work it and keep it" (Gen. 2:15). The verbs translated "work" and "keep" have priestly overtones of sacrifice and ministering the word of God. These same verbs are used together elsewhere in the books of Moses to describe only the work of the Levitical priests in the tabernacle (Num. 3:7–8; 8:26; 18:5–6).[14] Adam was intended to garden like a priest. He was to "keep" the sacred space of Eden from intruders, like unclean animals (Gen. 3:1; Lev. 11:42). Above all, however, he had to "keep" God's word (Ex. 20:6; Deut. 5:1; 1 Kings 9:6). If he had done so, he would have led creation to its seventh-day "rest" in God's glory.[15] Adam would have conducted the orchestra to God's glory the more deeply he kept to the song's melody. We would have drawn closer to God's song with our song response. The gift of song would be received liturgically. However, as we have seen, Adam plunged creation into disorder by seizing at the inheritance avariciously.

While God disinherited Adam and Israel, he nevertheless provided another way to receive the inheritance. The Law especially revealed how Israel could continue to meet with him through orderly, sacrificial worship—through liturgy. With the

---

14. G. K. Beale, *The Temple and the Church's Mission: A Biblical Theology of the Dwelling Place of God*, NSBT 17 (IVP Academic, 2004), 66–70; L. Michael Morales, *Who Shall Ascend the Mountain of the Lord? A Biblical Theology of the Book of Leviticus*, NSBT 37 (IVP Academic, 2015), 53.

15. There's already a hint of this in the verb rendered by the ESV as "put" (*nuah*); the clause might otherwise be translated loosely as "God rested him in the garden" (Gen. 2:15). See Beale, *The Temple and the Church's Mission*, 70.

old liturgy, God gave a foretaste of rest to his people in the ark and the temple, where he met them within created time (1 Kings 8:56; 1 Chron. 6:31; Ps. 132:8).[16] Above all, the Day of Atonement (Yom Kippur) was the annual occasion for Israel to realign the people, camp, sanctuary, and land with the song's doxological rhythm. Together, the people were to "afflict" themselves in repentance, turning again to the Lord who called them to himself with his word (Lev. 1:1; 16:29). It was the one time the high priest would go behind the veil to purify God's people so that God's glory could fill God's place in their midst (Lev. 9:23; 16:15). Hence, this day was a "Sabbath of solemn rest" (Lev. 16:31), connecting to God's "rest" on the seventh day (Gen. 2:2).[17]

Sabbath connections ripple outward from Yom Kippur, all pointing from the liturgy to God's rest. Yom Kippur fell on the Sabbath day of the Sabbath month.[18] Similarly, every seventh year would be a sabbatical year after the liturgy of Yom Kippur (Lev. 25:4), granting "solemn rest" to the land and its workers (Lev. 25:4–7). And every seventh sabbatical year, Jubilee proclaimed debts forgiven, inheritances of land returned, and the poor fed and redeemed from servitude (Lev. 25:8–55). These Sabbaths reminded Israel that creation belongs to God and can be received from his hands alone (Lev. 25:55). They therefore reasserted creation's doxological rhythm, which leads to God's rest and the created order in which they would receive it. Sabbaths were momentary foretastes of the inheritance creation was intended to be, and they were signal instances of how that inheri-

16. Further, and somewhat differently, Ephraim Radner, *Leviticus*, Brazos Theological Commentary on the Bible (Brazos, 2008), 237–56.

17. The ESV's "Sabbath of solemn rest" conveys the meaning of the original Hebrew, with a nod to the Septuagint. The Septuagint translates the Hebrew *shabbat shabbaton*, "Sabbath of Sabbaths," as *sabbata sabbatōn anapausis*, "a Sabbath of Sabbaths, a rest" (Lev. 16:31); cf. "rest" (*katapausis*) in Heb. 4:1–11.

18. See John W. Kleinig, *Leviticus*, Concordia Commentary (Concordia, 2003), 547–53.

tance would be received liturgically. But foretastes are not feasts, and shadows are not substances (Col. 2:17). They all pointed to something greater.

Christ's Fulfillment of the Liturgy

The promise of God's rest always anticipated an everlasting, "heavenly" fulfillment (Heb. 11:8–16).[19] Therefore, when we read that Jesus carries creation to its fulfillment "by the word of his power," it is because this word is the word of his cross (1 Cor. 1:18; Heb. 1:3). There is power in his blood to achieve what the old covenant sacrificial system could not: perfection and fulfillment (Heb. 7:11). In so doing, Jesus fulfills the old liturgy with a greater one and restores Adam's children to their priestly role as leaders of creation's praise.

The old liturgy was good, as far as it went. The problem was that it didn't go far enough to remedy the problem of humanity's sin and creation's consequent futility. The sacrificial rites of Yom Kippur would offer a momentary realignment of the land, community, and sanctuary with creation's doxological rhythm and order. These would cleanse the people (Lev. 16:30). But all this had an expiry date attached to it. The old liturgy was dependent on the blood of bulls and goats, which did not have the power to remove sins (Heb. 10:4). And the old priests were part of the problem they needed to remedy (Heb. 7:27–28).

Jesus's liturgy goes infinitely further than the old. He is the orchestra's new conductor, who leads it with something new and more promising. "Christ has obtained a ministry [*leitourgia*, "liturgy"] that is as much more excellent than the old as the covenant he mediates is better, since it is enacted on better promises" (Heb. 8:6). Jesus's ministry thus belongs to a "better

19. Ole Jakob Filtvedt, "Creation and Salvation in Hebrews," *Zeitschrift für die neutestamentliche Wissenschaft* 106, no. 2 (2015): 285–89.

covenant" (Heb. 7:22) with a "better hope" (Heb. 7:19), secures a "better word" of forgiveness (Heb. 12:24), brings us a "better possession" (Heb. 10:34), and makes us inheritors of a "better country" (Heb. 11:16).[20] Unlike the old sacrifices, his sacrifice is definitive and "once for all" (Heb. 10:10). With the blood of his own life-giving flesh, he enters the true holy places as our forerunner to purify and sanctify his people (Heb. 9:12). Christ's "blood of the eternal covenant" (Heb. 13:20) offered through the "eternal Spirit" (Heb. 9:14) wins an "eternal salvation," "eternal redemption," and "the promised eternal inheritance" for his people (Heb. 5:9; 9:12, 15). His shed blood therefore delivers us from the futility we inherited from Adam (1 Pet. 1:18–19) and restores us to our liturgical vocation with him, "to be a holy priesthood" (1 Pet. 2:5).

Jesus begins to undo the disorder of creation's orchestra by reordering its conductors alongside him. Through Jesus's death and resurrection, we now stand with him as he leads a hymn of praise to God "in the midst of the congregation" (Ps. 22:22; Heb. 2:12). He is not alone in his service but surrounded by "brothers" who have entered the holy places through him (Heb. 2:11). Though Jesus's ministry belongs to the "world to come" (Heb. 2:5), the church participates in it regularly when they gather to hear the word of God and receive the Lord's Supper. Heaven and earth, the future and the present, overlap in these moments. As the church gathers with angels and the heavenly assembly, they gather around God, the Judge of all things, and around Jesus, their mediator, to hear what God the Father hears in Jesus's liturgy: "the sprinkled blood that speaks a better word than the blood of Abel" (Heb. 12:24). They are hearing the "word" of Jesus's power, the same word that carries the universe to its end in God's rest. It is the word of Jesus's cross, on

20. John W. Kleinig, *Hebrews*, Concordia Commentary (Concordia, 2017), 394.

which he stretched out his arms to embrace the world's tensions and reconcile them in his body.

The Word through whom all things were created is also the Word of forgiveness and mercy. Those who receive God's word about what they are as creatures must also receive his word about who they are as brothers and sisters in the family of God. Creation longs for this. Where the Spirit gives faith to hear this word, he removes the disorder our sin unleashed upon creation and reasserts the Creator's order. The eternal light of the seventh day that radiates from the Lamb is like the Most Holy Place, and its glory has already shone on our hearts in anticipation of when it will shine upon our bodies (1 Cor. 15:43; 2 Cor. 4:6; Rev. 21:23). We have entered this holy place because Jesus's word makes us "clean" (John 15:3). Like Jubilee, the word of Christ proclaims our definitive forgiveness and freedom from sin's debt and enslaving power (Isa. 61:1–3; Matt. 11:2–6). His word therefore liberates us from futility and grants us a foretaste of eternal rest "today" (Heb. 4:7).

The Heart of Our Inheritance: God's Glory and Rest

Thus far we have examined the arrangement of God's creative song, revealed by the reprise of its melody that gathers all the song's various threads together to resolve them. The song's final movement reveals what its first movement always should have been. Unlike humanity's failure in Adam and Israel, Jesus is the faithful Son over the Father's household, appointed as its heir. And unlike the limited reach of the old liturgy, Jesus takes the orchestra to greater heights with his definitive priestly work. By fulfilling God's creative intention in our flesh and for us, he makes his brethren coheirs with him. We now have a taste of eternal rest in him. What do we inherit, and what is this rest? Our inheritance involves more than just the creation, because creation was never simply about itself.

Glory

In one sense, we inherit creation transfigured into the new heavens and new earth. This is the answer to the petition in our Lord's prayer that God's kingdom would "come" and his

> will be done
> on earth as it is in heaven. (Matt. 6:10)

When his kingdom has arrived in its fullness, it will be in the form of a new creation: "Then I saw a new heaven and a new earth, for the first heaven and the first earth had passed away, and the sea was no more" (Rev. 21:1). This new creation is connected to God's promise to "shake" heaven and earth (Hag. 2:6; Heb. 12:26). The earth shook when God warned Israel from the fire and angelic host at Sinai. Much more will it shake at Christ's return. This shaking will result in the "removal of things that are shaken—that is, things that have been made—in order that the things that cannot be shaken may remain" (Heb. 12:27). There is no idea of cosmic annihilation here. Some such misunderstanding may sometimes fuel rather mistaken approaches to how we relate to creation: Since God will burn it all down, we need not worry about beating him to the punch. That is not what God's judgment language suggests. Rather, God is promising to remove all that is unstable, transient, and standing in the way of fulfilling his creative intention. God will eliminate created things that prove shakable. What will remain is all that will pertain to God's counsel (Ps. 33:11), his righteousness and his praise (Ps. 111:3, 10), his truth (Ps. 117:2), and his word (Isa. 40:8), as well as David's offspring and his dominion (Ps. 89:36).[21] We see this in Isaiah's vision

21. Kleinig, *Hebrews*, 638, 661–63; see also Jihye Lee, *A Jewish Apocalyptic Framework of Eschatology in the Epistle to the Hebrews: Protology and Eschatology as Background*, LNTS 662 (T&T Clark, 2021), 128–30.

of the city of God, which gathers to itself the treasures of the nations that honor God (Isa. 60:1–22). Whatever remains in the new creation will harmonize completely with the song's melody, being full of God's glory (Hag. 2:7). And this includes the fruitfulness of our lives, our own harmonies with the Word.

The theme of God's glory is concerned with God's presence (Hag. 2:4–5; Zech. 2:5). God promised that his glory would fill the temple and he would dwell there with his people "forever" (Ezek. 43:7). The name of the new Jerusalem will be "The LORD Is There" (Ezek. 48:35). At the center of this new creation will be God himself, in his glorious presence with his people. "Behold, the dwelling place of God is with man. He will dwell with them, and they will be his people, and God himself will be with them as their God" (Rev. 21:3). In John's vision of the new creation, God's glory eclipses the temple altogether. "I saw no temple in the city, for its temple is the Lord God the Almighty and the Lamb. And the city has no need of sun or moon to shine on it, for the glory of God gives it light, and its lamp is the Lamb" (Rev. 21:22–23; cf. Isa. 60:20). Consequently, God's people will see his face, his glory, "and his servants will worship him" (Rev. 22:3–4).

The matter of the inheritance God's sons receive is not so straightforward, then. It involves the new creation, but for that very reason it necessarily involves God's glory. We have seen how creation's ultimate end is God's glory. This truth bears on our inheritance. Paul says that the Holy Spirit guarantees our status as God's children, and therefore as his heirs. He goes on to specify that we are "heirs of God and fellow heirs with Christ" (Rom. 8:17). Note well: We are heirs "of God"—God is our inheritance.[22] Paul connects this to being

22. Ivor J. Davidson, "Salvation's Destiny: Heirs of God," in *God of Salvation: Soteriology in Theological Perspective*, ed. Ivor J. Davidson and Murray A. Rae (Routledge, 2010), 154–75.

"glorified" with Jesus and clothed with glory in the resurrection (Rom. 8:18, 21–23, 30). Our inheritance is glorious because "of God."

As sons, we inherit creation because we inherit God's glory that fills it (Isa. 6:3). This is not because God hands over his glory. "My glory I give to no other," he says (Isa. 42:8). Rather, we inherit God's glory by participating in it. God unfolds his glory in creation to enfold us with it. "In your light do we see light" (Ps. 36:9). Through Christ, the song is resolved because we are drawn into the musicality of the Trinity's mutual glorification (John 17:24; cf. 12:28; 17:5). Creation comes to us because God comes to us with creative and glorifying love. Our inheritance is a gift that comes with the giver, but the primary gift is the giver himself.

Rest

When we inherit God as our portion and share in his glory, he crowns this inheritance with his own rest. The rest of the seventh day crowns the creation hymn's doxological rhythm. "God blessed the seventh day and made it holy, because on it God rested from all his work that he had done in creation" (Gen. 2:3). God's rest on the seventh day of creation is "for man" (Gen. 2:2–3; Mark 2:27). Unlike God's creative activity, we are invited and commanded to join God in his rest (Ex. 20:8–11).[23] But what is it?

In our day, we typically think of rest in terms of entertainment or inactivity. We seek to "escape" to other worlds, witness new things, and marvel at novelties. This is counterfeit rest, often rooted in despair with our lives and curiosity with the world's goods. At its core, rest as entertainment or escap-

23. Karl Barth, *Church Dogmatics*, 3/1, ed. G. W. Bromiley and T. F. Torrance, trans. J. W. Edwards et al. (T&T Clark, 1958), 225.

ism is a drug that inoculates us against reality. But the impulse that drives these counterfeits is a restlessness that can only rest in God. What these distractions seek is found in worship, where we meet with something infinitely different from ourselves, forever new, and weightier than the whole of reality: God in his glory.[24]

Rest is not mere inactivity, because it is a "Sabbath rest," involving worship (Heb. 4:9). This is not the mere interruption of work, for that leaves "rest" tethered to the possibilities of what work can provide, as well as its demands. This too characterizes our consumer culture, in which even our inactivity consists mainly of being sold all manner of things we can afford only through more and more work. "Rest" gets absorbed into the very things from which we need rest. It becomes preparation for further work.[25] But God's rest comes to us by grace. It is a gift inaccessible to work, transcending it (Heb. 4:10).

Sabbath rest is the freedom to actively glorify God with one's life and thereby rest in him. We find this rest in worship that receives God's word (Heb. 4:12–13). God prepared this rest from the "foundation of the world" by consecrating time and space to himself in worship (Heb. 4:3). In terms of time, the creation hymn already signals that this rest is perpetual and unceasing: The seventh "day" is not marked by the regular rhythm of morning and evening, beginning and end (Gen. 2:2–3). This is something unique. It is not the temporary rest afforded Israel in the land of Canaan (Deut. 12:10) but the everlasting fulfillment of created time in eternal life. Yet this rest is also the fulfillment of created space. It cannot be found in the temporary places where God chose to rest with his people, such

24. Josef Pieper, *In Tune with the World: A Theory of Festivity*, trans. Richard Winston and Clara Winston (St. Augustine's, 1999), 7, 58–59.

25. Making this point is Byung-Chul Han, *Vita Contemplativa: In Praise of Inactivity*, trans. Daniel Steuer (Polity, 2024).

as the land and the temple. God's "resting place forever" is in the heavenly Jerusalem (Ps. 132:13–14; Isa. 66:1–23).[26] Rest therefore belongs to the new heavens and new earth, where God dwells eternally with his people. And through Christ's liturgy, we "have come to Mount Zion and to the city of the living God, the heavenly Jerusalem," and therefore to a real participation in God's rest belonging to the new creation (Heb. 12:22). God's rest is the peaceful fellowship he enjoys with his people in eternal life, which is a participation in his triune musicality.

God gives us rest because God is rest in himself. God does not "rest" to recover from strenuous exertion. "He does not faint or grow weary" (Isa. 40:28). He rests to model for us the life-giving enjoyment of his own goodness and bounty.[27] After all, nothing short of God can quiet our restless hearts. David says,

> You are my Lord;
> I have no good apart from you. (Ps. 16:2)

And in his presence "there is fullness of joy," which we receive by inheriting the Lord as our portion (Pss. 16:11; cf. 21:6; cf. Num. 18:20). God loves and enjoys his own goodness, which is partly why Scripture calls him "blessed" (1 Tim. 6:15). God's rest is therefore different from ordinary rest because he rests in himself. He is the eternal peace and blessedness from which all peace and blessedness come.

Resting from his works, God teaches us not only that we will have to rest from our own works but also that we will

26. For context, see Kleinig, *Hebrews*, 211–19; Craig Koester, *Hebrews: A New Translation with Introduction and Commentary*, The Anchor Bible 36 (Doubleday, 2001), 267–81.

27. God's rest in Gen. 2:2–3 is really his "abstention from work," which gets anthropomorphized into themes of rest and refreshment later (Ex. 20:11; 31:17). See Umberto Cassuto, *Commentary on the Book of Genesis*, pt. 1, *From Adam to Noah*, trans. Israel Abrahams (Magnes, 1961), 63.

have to rest in him (Ps. 116:7; Jer. 6:16). We will have to rest in God as God rests in himself so that we "might be well off in him, through him, and for him."[28] So, when God is "refreshed" from his rest, this signifies that God delights in himself (Ex. 31:17). Ordinary rest refreshes us because it enables us to recover our strength (2 Sam. 16:14). But this is a picture of something more, for it is ultimately God who strengthens us (Ps. 28:7; 2 Cor. 12:10; Phil. 4:13). God is the source of all strength and rest, with no source above him. Therefore, "the refreshment of the saints and of God is the same. . . . God is refreshed in the enjoyment of his own self."[29] We too are refreshed in the enjoyment of God.

Just as God welcomes us into his glory, so he welcomes us into his rest. As its faithful liturgist, Jesus leads creation to this end. The Son who is the "radiance of the glory of God" leads "many sons to glory" (Heb. 1:3; 2:10). The heir and builder of the Father's household can give it the "rest" of God's presence and freedom from all threats (Heb. 3:1–14; 4:1–10; 6:19–20). Adam was meant to be crowned "with glory and honor" (Ps. 8:5), but he left his posterity a crown of "thorns and thistles" (Gen. 3:18). So Jesus takes the thistle crown, that we may receive the honor crown. Like Israel, we were meant to rest in the promised land but got lost in the wilderness (Ps. 95:7–11). So Jesus goes into the wilderness, that we may receive God's rest there (Matt. 4:1; 11:28). Meeting us amid our exile and wandering, Jesus brings us glory and rest with his word. "Let us therefore strive to enter that rest" (Heb. 4:11). The song's melody of glory and rest comes to us in and through our high priest's liturgy. We may now receive the song we were meant to inherit. This happens to us now by hearing the melody of

28. Robert Grosseteste, *On the Six Days of Creation*, trans. C. F. J. Martin (Oxford University Press, 1996), 9.3.4 (277).

29. Aquinas, *Commentary on the Psalms* 49.495.

the Word and responding to it with song of our own in confession and in prayer (Heb. 4:14, 16). We do so in the company of many brothers and sisters, as a witness to the world of the common doxology that will eventually overtake the nations and every creature.

Conclusion

Christ resolves the song's tensions and reveals the glorious harmony in which it will rest. Those who came before this revelation longed to hear what we have heard, but they "did not hear it" (Matt. 13:17). We can sympathize with this longing when we mourn over the puzzling features of our lives marked by futility, sorrow, and pain. It can often feel as if this world were mere noise, not song. Naturally we wonder why we suffer and why God seems so far from us (Ps. 13). Is God's creation going anywhere, much less our individual lives?

When we are faced with such questions, it is paramount to remember that while Christ reveals the song's arrangement, we cannot grasp it wholly until he returns. We have yet to hear all of the song's final movement, even if we have heard its central melody. Our examples, therefore, are the saints who went before us. Even though they did not hear the movements of the song we have, they nevertheless clung in faith to the bit of the melody they had heard, the Creator's promise (Heb. 11:39–40). Apart from us, they would not be perfected. And apart from the saints to come and the assembly of the firstborn in heaven, neither will we (Heb. 12:22–24). As the examples of these saints show us, faith lives not by sight but by the power of God's invisible speech, which can create and reorder all things (Heb. 11:3). We do not yet see all things subject to Christ (Heb. 2:8). So we must believe without having seen (John 20:29–31). We do not yet hear the whole "new song" the angels sing (Rev. 14:3). So we must let the word of Christ dwell richly in our hearts, that we might sing "with angels and archangels, and with all the company of heaven" (see Col. 3:16).[30]

30. Book of Common Prayer 1662, preface to the Eucharistic prayer.

7

"I Will Sing and Make Melody to the Lord"

Gratitude and Sacrifice

Hearing the "better word" of Jesus's blood, we hear the song's resolution (Heb. 12:24). Creation came from God and is now moving back to him so that he may be "all in all" (1 Cor. 15:28). The dissonance we had caused in creation's liturgy is now being overcome by the new song of Jesus Christ, who cleanses us with the word of his cross and gathers us to himself as a kingdom of priests who serve with him. As priests covered with his anointing (Song 1:3), we are now restored to our vocation as conductors of creation's praise.

The song's resolution tells us what this vocation will look like in the end, giving us clues about what it should look like now. For the word of Christ is unbound by tomorrow or yesterday; it reaches us today (Heb. 4:7; 13:8). It tells us that Isaiah's vision of God's throne room as a cosmic space is unfolding before our eyes with the doxological rhythm of Christ's new song (Isa. 6:1–5). John portrays this vision with strongly sacrificial overtones. Nothing "unclean" (Rev. 21:27) or "accursed"—set apart for destruction (Rev. 22:3; cf. Lev. 27:29; Deut. 7:26)—will enter the new Jerusalem. Before God's throne "his servants will worship him" (Rev. 22:3), and his name will be on their foreheads, signaling their liturgical consecration to him (Num. 6:27; Rev. 22:4; 3:12). God's throne will no longer be a place separated from the creation, hidden behind veils and rites to protect us. Rather, we will be perpetually before God's throne and so will "serve him day and night in his temple" (Rev. 7:15). Our consecration to God in worship will embrace our whole lives in the new creation, sheltered by God's glory. The eternal flame of the Lamb illuminates our way through life and death into unceasing glory (Rev. 21:23). This, the true last syllable of recorded time, stretches into our lives now and summons us forward. Our opportunity to sing has been given back to us. How then should we use this opportunity? What is the doxological life, resonant with the Creator's music?

As we must now see in conclusion, the doxological life fulfills Adam's original vocation. It is oriented by the vision of the new creation, which restores our royal and priestly calling to "reign" over creation and to serve God. We must therefore consider (1) the meaning of human dominion and (2) how sacrifice defines the proper use of creation.

Royal Dominion: Receiving Creation with Gratitude

Any discussion of human dominion over creation requires a sense of both humor and humility. After all, the two have a kinship. Both play their proper role when God's dominion is set forth as the wider context for human dominion. Because creatures are gifts given from God, all creatures belong to God, not to themselves. God is the "Possessor of heaven and earth" (Gen. 14:22) such that he can say, "All the earth is mine" (Ex. 19:5). David confesses,

> The earth is the LORD's and the fullness thereof,
> the world and those who dwell therein. (Ps. 24:1)

And God explains to his people why he does not benefit from their sacrifices:

> For every beast of the forest is mine,
> the cattle on a thousand hills.
> I know all the birds of the hills,
> and all that moves in the field is mine.
>
> If I were hungry, I would not tell you,
> for the world and its fullness are mine. (Ps. 50:10–12)

Since everything belongs to God, it is therefore his to give (Gen. 9:3; Ps. 115:16). However, the gifts of this world, its creatures, and even ourselves are inseparable from the giver who can give them without giving them away. To receive God's gifts is not thereby to have full control over them, to do with them as we please. It always remains that "we are *gardeners* of someone else's garden."[1] We must answer for what we do with God's gifts, dominion included. Two immediate consequences follow. First, since God gives gifts differently than anyone else, he can give creation to humanity without surrendering it as his possession. Our dominion is therefore relative, not absolute—an image engraved upon mortal flesh, not the everlasting archetype. Second, we must receive the gifts God gives. Ordinary experience is full of tricky negotiations

1. Robert W. Jenson, *Systematic Theology*, vol. 2, *The Works of God* (Oxford University Press, 2001), 2:115.

with gifts: They can be given without much thought for the recipient; we can wonder about the motives of those who give them, whether they come with strings and "debts" attached; and even when they're appropriately given, we risk their poor reception. None of these disorderly dynamics are in play with God's gifts. We need not fear that God is manipulating us when giving us gifts, for down that path is the irreverence and ingratitude that blinds itself to God's generosity (Rom. 1:21). The proper answer to a real gift is gratitude, for this is how gifts are fully received.[2] And so too with our dominion, which must be received actively in the ways God dictates. That is, we must receive God's gifts in a way that befits what those gifts are.

These reflections on God's gift giving and our gratitude give dominion a distinctive flavor. No sooner does Scripture announce human dominion than it provides a test exposing what it looks like when Adam names the animals and searches for an appropriate "helper" from God (Gen. 2:18). This episode shows us what human dominion looks like writ large. To say that naming something expresses authority over it, as many accounts of this episode do, is to say both too little and too much. Naming the animals is not like branding them—and neither is Adam's naming of his wife (Gen. 2:23; 3:20)! Rather, in Scripture, naming declares the nature of things and their character. For instance, the names Cain and Abel already foreshadow their place in the unfolding of God's song (Gen. 4:1–2). These names mysteriously point us to the truth of these persons. Eve names her firstborn Cain, which rhymes with a word for "create," signaling the looming temptation of pride within her pro-

2. Kenneth L. Schmitz, *The Gift: Creation* (Marquette University Press, 1982), 47–48. In his detailed account of thankfulness, Peter J. Leithart, *Gratitude: An Intellectual History* (Baylor University Press, 2014) describes how Christianity introduced the notion of gratitude as the proper reception and use of gifts.

creative power and the life that comes from it (cf. Deut. 32:6; Ps. 139:13).[3] Likewise, Abel is from the word translated "vanity," "breath," or "vapor," ominously speaking to the brevity of his life (Job 7:16; Ps. 144:4; Eccl. 1:2). Names are not arbitrary signifiers in Scripture.

With this in mind, we may understand what Adam's naming of animals tells us about receiving God's gifts with gratitude. As a royal priest in the garden, Adam is supposed to "work it and keep it" (Gen. 2:15), which concerns his liturgical commission to keep God's word by obeying it and ordering all else to it (Deut. 5:1). The task of naming involves careful attentiveness and wisdom, perceiving the God-given nature of things, and thereby knowing their place within God's song. In other words, Adam must hear creatures as words of God's creative speech. Hearing them as words, he understands them as the whole things God speaks into being, which are meant to harmonize with God's Word and function within the created order in relation to God and to other creatures.[4] According to Luther, Adam "views all the animals and thus arrives at such a knowledge of their nature that he can give each one a suitable name that harmonizes with its nature."[5]

The first act of Adam's unique relation to creation, his dominion, is to study it scrupulously. The orchestra's conductor learns the different families of instruments, their individual parts, and the unique sounds each can produce. He attends to each creature's particularity, drawing near to discover its

3. These associations are difficult to hear in most English translations. To draw them out, we might translate the passage as follows: "Adam knew his wife Eve, and she conceived and gave birth to Cain [*qayin*]. Then she said, 'I have created [*qaniti*] a man with the LORD!'" (Gen. 4:1). The phrase "with the LORD" is ambiguous, serving as a factual description of Eve's proximity to the very creative power of God, but with a hint of the potential for this proximity to degenerate into pride.

4. See here, once again, chap. 4, under "Hearing What God's Creative Word Speaks" (p. 85).

5. Martin Luther, *Lectures on Genesis*, chaps. 1–5 (*LW* 1:119).

individual nuances and details.[6] While many early commentators in Christian tradition held that the naming took place quickly, it's not unreasonable to imagine a longer undertaking. Scripture doesn't force our hand either way. The important thing to recognize is how the scene instructs us about Adam's relation to the rest of the world, which is, above all, concerned with wisdom.

The fact that Adam must name animals represents something larger than labeling things. This scene fits into a broader pattern within Scripture, where animals and the natural features of this world are figures for what wisdom can teach us. The naming episode instructs us in receiving God's gifts with wisdom. Hence, Scripture commends the study of animals to us:

> Go to the ant, O sluggard;
> consider her ways, and be wise.
> Without having any chief,
> officer, or ruler,
> she prepares her bread in summer
> and gathers her food in harvest. (Prov. 6:6–8)

> The lizard you can take in your hands,
> yet it is in kings' palaces. (Prov. 30:28)

The righteous man is

> like a tree
> planted by streams of water
> that yields its fruit in its season,
> and its leaf does not wither. (Ps. 1:3)

6. The emphasis on proximity for discovering particularity emerges especially in Adam's poetic response to the creation of woman, where he thrice repeats the pronoun "this" (*zot*): "This [*zot*] at last is bone of my bones / and flesh of my flesh; / she [*zot*] shall be called Woman, / because she [*zot*] was taken out of Man" (Gen. 2:23). Adam's attentive proximity to Eve enables his discovery of her.

Jesus sends his disciples out "as sheep in the midst of wolves," who are to "be wise as serpents and innocent as doves" (Matt. 10:16). And so on. More ominously, God chastises Israel for being dumber than beasts:

> The ox knows its owner,
> and the donkey its master's crib,
> but Israel does not know,
> my people do not understand. (Isa. 1:3)

Calvin comments that God sends us to the "school of beasts" to learn better our duty, "for beasts often pursue the order of nature better, and exhibit more humanity than humans themselves."[7] Bavinck also draws lessons from the similarity of apes and humans, arguing that the ape presents to us a "caricature" of what we are without "the spirit that is from above."[8] Nonhuman creatures are parables of wisdom, allegorizing its truths in their created shapes.[9] Christian tradition is full of approaches to Scripture that seek to learn the allegorical depths of creatures for the sake of living wisely and righteously in God's creation.[10] God speaks wisdom to us through other creatures to guide us to himself:

7. John Calvin, *Commentary on Isaiah* 1:3 (*CO* 36:30).

8. Herman Bavinck, *Our Reasonable Faith*, trans. Henry Zylstra (Eerdmans, 1956), 201.

9. See, further, Robert M. Grant, *Early Christians and Animals* (Routledge, 1999). Ephraim Radner, *Leviticus*, Brazos Theological Commentary on the Bible (Brazos, 2008), 46–47, likens Scripture's perspective on animals to medieval bestiaries (see also 115–19). Paul M. Blowers, *The Drama of the Divine Economy: Creator and Creation in Early Christian Theology and Piety* (Oxford University Press, 2012), 213–72, discusses the broader scope of patristic "natural contemplation" and its place within the church's doxology. The works of Norman Wirzba, whom I have engaged occasionally, can be understood as a modern example of such natural contemplation.

10. One of the leading examples here is Basil of Caesarea's *Homilies on the Hexaemeron*. For another example, the English Puritan Edward Leigh, *A Systeme or Body of Divinity: Consisting of Ten Books* (London, 1662), bk. 3, chaps. 3–6 (290–335), speaks at length about elements and minerals, thunder and clouds, rains and winds, as well as the heavenly bodies and different kinds of fish, fowl, insects, and beasts. While he makes certain observations using the natural philosophy of his day, he also comments (albeit sparingly) on how attending to things like trees instructs us about living for God's glory.

> Ask the beasts, and they will teach you;
> the birds of the heavens, and they will tell you;
> or the bushes of the earth, and they will teach you;
> and the fish of the sea will declare to you. (Job 12:7–8)

All these know basic truths of wisdom we are prone to suppress (Rom. 1:18). Naming the animals, Adam exemplifies the pursuit of wisdom for the sake of receiving God's gifts faithfully. In so many words, he receives the animals as gifts as he receives wisdom about the created order through them.

Adam's task is therefore to become wise about the world, like Solomon, who will speak "of trees . . . of beasts, and of birds, and of reptiles, and of fish" (1 Kings 4:33). This wisdom is eminently practical. Knowing how creatures relate to God informs Adam about how he should relate to other creatures. They are given to him and subjected to him, of course. But their existence transcends being useful for his purposes. As Job is reminded in the whirlwind, the hidden ways and purposes of nonhuman creatures concern God's glory chiefly (Job 38–41). Creatures have their own integrity apart from human designs. Indeed, as they parade before Adam, he can name them only as he exemplifies the "respect for life" that must accompany all his interactions with creatures.[11] He discerns their names by respecting their freedom and integrity as God's creatures, not his playthings.[12] He knows that God, not his belly, governs the meaning and ends of all creatures—himself included (cf. Phil. 3:19). Just as he must distinguish all the garden's trees from one of them, so too this task requires distinctions (Gen. 2:16–17). He must distinguish the natures and ends of creatures from the range of human purposes they can serve, so he draws near to

11. Karl Barth, *Church Dogmatics*, 3/4, ed. G. W. Bromiley and T. F. Torrance, trans. A. T. MacKay et al. (T&T Clark, 1961), 324–97.

12. Cf. J. G. Hamann, *Aesthetica in nuce*, in *Hamann: Writings on Philosophy and Language*, ed. Kenneth Hayne (Cambridge University Press, 2007), 78.

the creatures and discovers the scope and limits of their service to him within their service to God.[13] Such acts of attentiveness and discovery are implicit in his role as a gardener.[14] These also lead him to expect the "help" befitting his unique nature and dignity to come from another (Gen. 2:20).[15]

While much more could be said about all this, two takeaways will suffice for our purposes. First, we need wisdom to receive God's gifts. Indeed, wisdom is one of the primary gifts God gives (James 1:5, 17). It is the open hand toward the whole creation and other creatures that begins and ends in openness to God. "The Lord by wisdom founded the earth," and it is by wisdom that we inhabit that world as we ought (Prov. 3:19; cf. Ps. 104:24). Wisdom attunes us to the Creator's song, making us aware of the world around us, ourselves, and our days.[16] It's part of the song's melody that comes into our hearts and delights our souls (Prov. 2:10). It alerts us to the natures and ends of creatures within God's purposes, which provide the broader contours of how other creatures may or may not fit into human purposes.

Second, it follows that wisdom enables gratitude, which is the proper reception and use of God's gifts. With our confession

13. Recall the discussion of purposes and ends in chap. 2, under "Why God Opens His Musicality" (p. 52).

14. Norman Wirzba, *Food and Faith: A Theology of Eating*, 2nd ed. (Cambridge University Press, 2019), 75–103.

15. The woman Eve is described as a "helper" who is "fit for" or "corresponding to" man, implying both sexual difference and suitability—the kind needed for fruitfulness (Gen. 2:18; cf. 1:28). Following suggestions by David W. Cotter, *Genesis*, Berit Olam (Liturgical Press, 2003), 31–33, two observations are in order. First, God is the one who will provide this helper, and when God provides "help," it is typically for overcoming the threat of death (Ex. 18:4; Deut. 33:7, 26–29). This strongly suggests that Eve will help Adam overcome the threat of death that his solitude and fruitlessness would otherwise pose. Second, strength and help from God are parallel in Scripture (Ps. 46:1; cf. the meanings of the names Azariah and Uzziah, the same king, in 2 Kings 14:21 and 2 Chron. 26:1). This too suggests that, as Adam's "helper," Eve will have her own different kind of "strength" corresponding to his (Prov. 31:17, 25)—one weaker when compared with his physical strength (1 Pet. 3:7), but different and necessary for human life and fecundity.

16. Oliver O'Donovan, *Self, World, and Time*, Ethics as Theology 1 (Eerdmans, 2013), 1–19.

of God as Creator, Christians understand that everything we have is a gift from God (1 Cor. 4:7). He is the main recipient of our gratitude. Thankfulness is therefore not simply an attitude or the act of repaying the benefactor for his gifts. It consists rather in a moral, "attentive receptivity" toward God for his gifts.[17] Gratitude describes how we receive gifts with love. Properly ordered love is aligned with the created order, the natures and ends of things within their mutual order to one another and their ultimate ordering to God. Where these things are properly discerned, we will know how to use the things of creation with love that answers God's love. After all, to be a creature is to remain indebted to God for his gifts. Even when all other debts are settled, we still carry a debt of love (Rom. 13:8). Insofar as we receive other creatures from God's hands, we receive them gratefully with love that extends to God and neighbor.

Human dominion looks like understanding the world as God's, and therefore ours in a subordinate sense that is responsible to God. This responsibility demands wisdom and gratitude. We may gather creation's goods together wisely when we receive them with thanksgiving, using them in the service of God and our neighbor. But this is possible only where we acknowledge that while created goods are for our benefit, they must not be reduced to our benefit. They exist chiefly, like all things, for the glory of God—this is their opportunity to sing. Knowing this, we may then consider whether and how to use creatures for our benefit.

Dominion goes awry where we have not first perceived creatures as the Creator's poetry—as words of the Word, parts of his song. This truth is difficult to hear under the sway of rationalistic and scientistic approaches to the things of this world, which tend to result in either a domineering abuse of creation or

17. Schmitz, *The Gift*, 47.

a romanticizing divinization of it. Creation is neither a godless wasteland nor the body of God. Both errors are common. On the one hand, creation becomes a sacred object for our veneration. Consequently, the world is approached as an idol rather than something to be received with wisdom in service of God and neighbor. On the other hand, creation becomes a world of objects for our experimental gaze and technological manipulation. Our orientation to the world becomes dominated by the lust for mastery and control. The concept of human dominion over creation is often bemoaned and blamed for these latter misuses, especially in theologies sensitive to ecological concerns. But poor use doesn't rule out good use. No doubt, experimentation and technology are ways of exercising dominion over creation. Much good comes to us through the disciplines of chemistry and physics, as with careful use of creatures to good purpose, like when we employ them for food and clothing. Faithfulness depends on whether we do this with true wisdom and gratitude. When using creatures, we must ask how our use respects their natures and ends and how it serves to love God and neighbor.

Priestly Use: Consecrating Creation for Sacrifice

Thus far, we have explored what dominion looks like when we remember that everything belongs to God—even our dominion. As Adam worked the ground, he was to do so with wisdom and thankfulness to God, mindful of the Creator's provision. However, this also meant that he was to tend the ground sacrificially, gratefully and wholeheartedly devoting to God the fruits of God's generosity. This intention is echoed in the religious feasts marking creation's doxological rhythm, where the Creator's bounty is enjoyed and shared as it is brought to him in praise (Lev. 23). Intrinsic to Adam's liturgical commission, therefore, was a sacrificial disposition toward the Creator. This is what we see immediately after the garden, in the sacrifices of Cain and Abel. Whereas Cain merely brought the "fruit of the ground," Abel brought an offering "of the firstborn of his flock and of their fat portions" (Gen. 4:3–4). Abel offered the most precious fruits of the Lord's gifts to him, for which reason God regards Abel and his offering favorably. The proper use of God's gifts requires sacrifice. But what exactly is a sacrifice?

We're typically very mistaken about sacrifice, which we consider a rather gloomy concept. It is as if all sacrifice amounted to is discarding something wastefully. Or perhaps we believe it means giving something up, foregoing or abandoning it, to court favor with deities who morbidly take pleasure in our discomfort. But this is not what sacrifice means. The old covenant sacrifices were always signs and tokens of the inward sacrifice of the worshiper. God critiqued the sacrifices of the old covenant when they were merely outward offerings divorced from the interior sacrifice of "a broken and contrite heart" devoted to him and conformed to his character (Ps. 51:16–17; cf. 50:12–15; Mic. 6:6–8). God instructs us through his prophet that he desires

> steadfast love and not sacrifice,
> the knowledge of God rather than burnt offerings.
> (Hos. 6:6)

Without obedience and conformity to God's will, sacrifices are empty (1 Sam. 15:22). The old covenant sacrifices are fulfilled in Christ's sacrifice, for they all anticipate his sacrificial "body" (Col. 2:17 KJV; Heb. 10:5). Sacrifice has consequently been spiritualized, bringing its interior dimension to the fore (Luke 11:41–42).[18] But this isn't the same as divorcing sacri-

18. Everett Ferguson, "Spiritual Sacrifice in Early Christianity and Its Environment," in *Aufstieg und Niedergang der römischen Welt*, pt. 2, *Principat*, 23.2, ed. Hildegard Temporini and Wolfgang Haase (De Gruyter, 1980), 1151–89.

fice from its exterior aspect in life—the material things of this world and our use of them. Hence, the author of Hebrews encourages the church to "continually offer up a sacrifice of praise to God" through Christ. Such sacrifice is "the fruit of lips that acknowledge his name," and it looks like good works and generosity. "Such sacrifices are pleasing to God" (Heb. 13:15–16; cf. Phil. 4:18).

For such reasons, we may, with Augustine, understand sacrifice as "every act done in order that we might cling to God in holy fellowship, that is, every act which is referred to the final good in which we can be truly blessed."[19] In this definition, the many kinds of sacrifice in the old covenant are signs of the different shapes that love of God and neighbor take. True sacrifice is "to make sacred" (*sacrum facere*) the created goods of this life. Things are made sacred when devoted to God and his purposes, when God's gifts are consecrated to his service. Having consecrated them, we then use them to worship him, meaning that the end for which we use them is God's glory rather than our own. The opposite of true sacrifice co-opts God's gifts for our own vain purposes and effectively makes mere creatures recipients of religious devotion and consecration, which is the same as idolizing ourselves and others. Instead, we must remember that only God receives sacrifices, even though they do not benefit him. Sacrifice displays how God's gifts are received in gratitude and used doxologically, such that God's glory is manifest in and through our obedience (Lev. 9:23; 2 Cor. 9:13).

At the heart of this Augustinian definition of sacrifice is Jesus's own act of offering himself out of love (John 13:1). Christ's whole human life is defined by the sacrificial "form of a servant" (Phil. 2:7). Jesus consecrated himself as a sacrifice

19. Augustine, *City of God* 10.6 (trans. William Babcock, *WSA* I/6:310). See also Radner, *Leviticus*, 287–99.

so that his church would be consecrated for sacrificial service through him (John 17:17–19; Heb. 10:10). Human life conformed to the Word in the power of the Spirit therefore takes the shape of a "living sacrifice" (Rom. 12:1; cf. 1 Pet. 2:5). And since this includes our whole life in its temporal and spatial shape, then to bring ourselves to God as living sacrifices is to gather everything in our lives into the service of God. The church is where this happens most conspicuously, which is why it is a kingdom of priests, holy unto God (Ex. 19:6; 1 Pet. 2:9). Our approach to ourselves, our world, and our time is characterized not only by royal dominion but also by priestly consecration and sacrifice.

As we reflect on the way that sacrifice completes our gratitude to God for his gifts, animals are once again a window into the broader contours of how we should use all God's gifts. Specifically, we may look at the way animals figured into laws governing sacrifice and dietary restrictions. These laws help us see how God's gifts are consecrated for the sacrifice of praise that characterizes our priestly role as creation's liturgists. To use animals and other living creatures in sacrificial worship, Israel had to distinguish between the common and the holy, the clean and the unclean (Lev. 10:10–11). Some creatures could be offered to God, and others could not. The reason for this was not any intrinsic qualities making some animals better than others. Rather, the distinction teaches us how worship pervades our whole life and how we interact with other creatures. This is particularly visible in the dietary laws downstream from the basic distinction between unclean and clean animals (Lev. 11).[20]

The dietary laws are not the same within the new covenant as they were in the old, but they continue to instruct us

20. On this, see especially John W. Kleinig, *Leviticus*, Concordia Commentary (Concordia, 2003), 256–60.

about how we, as priests of creation's praise, approach other creatures. Animals like pigs were unclean but did not transmit that impurity until they were dead and misused. The liturgy distinguished good use from misuse. This is an important point for understanding how categories like pure and impure continue to function in the new covenant. Unclean animals could not be consecrated to God sacrificially. To approach God in sacrifice with humility, reverence, and gratitude required that worshipers be mindful of treating God's creatures according to his word.

This truth about using creatures according to God's word and for his glory remains in force in the new covenant. The old dietary laws distinguished Israel from the surrounding nations (Lev. 18:24; 20:22–27). In this respect, these same laws are fulfilled—not annulled—by Christ's gathering of the Gentiles into his church (Mark 7:1–23; Acts 10:9–16; 15:20). Corresponding to the bountiful riches of God's grace toward Jews and Gentiles is the Lord's bounty in creation. "Nothing is unclean in itself" (Rom. 14:14). Now the only dietary practices that distinguish the people of God from the world are those testifying to God's lordship and the moral purity befitting the body of Christ, since the church partakes of the Lord's Supper (Acts 15:20, 28; 1 Cor. 11:27–32).[21] The issue of ritual purity has now been focused on the matter of spiritual purity, for our bodies are now temples of the Holy Spirit. In the new covenant, God's people are defined not by what they do not eat but by what they do eat: the body and blood of Christ. Just so, we must continue to distinguish

21. To partake of the Lord's Supper in an "unworthy manner" is to participate without "discerning the body" of Christ (1 Cor. 11:27, 29). The "body" in question is the corporate body Christ has made pure by his word (John 15:3; 1 Cor. 10:16–18). Living an unclean life makes one unworthy to receive the Supper, for an unrepentant and wayward soul approaches the table proclaiming something other than the purity of Christ's body and the efficacy of his blood. An image of this is Judas, who receives the first Supper having already determined in his heart to betray the Lord, after which Satan "enters into" him (John 13:2, 27).

clean and unclean things for the sake of worship. Hence, things can still *become* unclean when not used with faith that works by love for God and neighbor (Rom. 14:13–23).

Christ's liturgical fulfillment of creation therefore does not set aside but intensifies the distinction between clean and unclean things. What is clean and unclean depends on what comes from the heart and the conscience. Unclean things will have no place in the new creation (Rev. 21:7–8, 22–27). But to those who have been made clean and pure by God's word, "all things are pure" (Titus 1:15). And what is clean and pure can be consecrated to the Lord's service, provided we are mindful of our neighbor's needs (1 Cor. 10:23–11:1). When we receive God's gifts with gratitude, we may use the things of this world and our lives sacrificially, bringing them before the Lord (Ps. 96:8). Food and all other created goods can and must be consecrated to the Lord's service because God has made us, his priests, clean. Since priests handle holy things, we must make holy our lives, the goods of this world, and our days in the service of God.[22]

False teachers, following unclean spirits and demons, advocate the misuse of God's good gifts. For instance, they may disparage created institutions like marriage or promote abstinence from certain foods (1 Tim. 4:1–3). The church's response to these false views is to remember creation's goodness and our priestly vocation within it. "Everything created by God is good, and nothing is to be rejected if it is received with thanksgiving, for it is made holy by the word of God and prayer" (1 Tim. 4:4–5). God created all things good, which means they are intrinsically good and delightful to God and are fit for showing forth his glory. They are therefore not to be rejected but welcomed with the hospitality of wisdom. Created

22. Cf. Leithart, *Gratitude*, 72.

goods are received with gratitude only "by those who believe and know the truth" about the good Creator and his good creation (1 Tim. 4:3). This means receiving them as the good things God's Word creates them to be, "clean" and therefore fit for his service (Gen. 1:31; Mark 7:19). With this "song" of thanksgiving, we consecrate ourselves and our world unto God (Ps. 69:30). Created goods are thereby taken up into the movement of sacrifice that makes them holy, for "the one who offers thanksgiving as his sacrifice glorifies" God (Ps. 50:23). We ask God in faith to bless the sacrificial use of his gifts. Prayer acknowledges that while we have no right of ourselves to use any of God's gifts, we do have God's promise, which makes us heirs of creation and its goods.[23] When all things are thus sanctified by the word of God and prayer, gratitude becomes "the liturgy of Christian living."[24]

Sacrifice is not the annihilation of created goods but the doxological use of them to the glory of God. Sacrifice is also contrary to an unyielding possessiveness over created goods, an unchaste love for them. Consecrating things means that we do not cherish them more than God, just as a loving wife would not cherish her wedding ring more than her beloved husband.[25] In this respect we can speak moderately about "contempt" for the world compared with God when created goods stand in the way of or compete with our love for God (see Mark 10:21–22; John 12:25).[26]

23. John Calvin, *Commentary on 1 Timothy* 4:5 (CO 52:297).

24. Leithart, *Gratitude*, 72.

25. Bonaventure, *Commentary on Ecclesiastes*, vol. 7 of *Works of St. Bonaventure* (Franciscan Institute, 2005), 78: "This world is like a ring given by the bridegroom to the soul itself. Now the bride can love the ring given her by her husband in two ways, namely, with *a chaste* or *an adulterous* love. The love is *chaste* when she loves the ring as a memento of her husband and on account of her love for her husband. The love is *adulterous* when the ring is loved more than the husband, and the husband cannot regard such love as good. . . . Contempt for a ring by treating it as a poor and ugly gift reflects on the husband, but contempt of a ring by regarding it as almost nothing compared to the love of a husband, gives glory to the husband."

26. Augustine, *Expositions of the Psalms* 148.15 (trans. Maria Boulding, *WSA* III/20:574): "Whatever among all these things gives you pleasure is less than God himself.

But there can be no such thing as a principled scornfulness toward creation, as if it were not God's good song. Sacrifice instead shows us that everything we have is a gift meant to draw us closer to God through devoting it and ourselves to him. Our own created lives can be received as the gifts they are not by preserving them at all costs but only by giving them back to God in sacrifice. "For whoever would save his life will lose it, but whoever loses his life for my sake will find it" (Matt. 16:25); "For none of us lives to himself, and none of us dies to himself. For if we live, we live to the Lord, and if we die, we die to the Lord. So then, whether we live or whether we die, we are the Lord's" (Rom. 14:7–8).

Conclusion

The church's sacrificial activity consecrates it and the world to sing the common doxology of creation's orchestra. To offer "sacrifices with shouts of joy" in the Lord's presence is to "sing and make melody to the Lord" (Ps. 27:6). In this way, we "take up the psaltery" of a good life that pleases God (see Pss. 147:11; 149:4). While anyone's ears can delight in a song, God's "ears are sensitive not to the mouth but to the heart, not to the tongue but to the life of the one who praises him."[27] A life of sacrifice beats with the rhythm and order of God's original song, which is completed in his new song. This is the shape of life in harmony with the Word. Christ's sacrifice frees us from futility to receive God's gifts gratefully and to wonder at God's generosity. It is an awesome thing that God would give this world to his children

---

Do not allow your pleasure in what he has made, therefore, to lure you away from him who made it; rather, if you love what he has made, love the maker far more. If the things he has made are so beautiful, how much more beautiful must he be who made them?" See also Aquinas, *Summa theologiae* I-II, q. 109, a. 3.

27. Augustine, *Expositions of the Psalms* 146.3 (Boulding, *WSA* III/20:496).

as our inheritance, that he would lavish upon us such gifts for our use. Yet more awesome still is that God would give himself. God glorifies himself with sacrifice so that we may sing with all creatures,

> To him who sits on the throne and to the Lamb
> be blessing and honor and glory and might forever
> and ever! (Rev. 5:13)

> Why are we by all creatures waited on?
> Why do the prodigal elements supply
> Life and food to me, being more pure than I,
> Simple, and further from corruption?
> Why brooks't thou, ignorant horse, subjection?
> Why dost thou, bull and boar, so sillily
> Dissemble weakness, and by one man's stroke die,
> Whose whole kind you might swallow and feed upon?
> Weaker I am, woe is me, and worse than you,
> You have not sinn'ed, nor need be timorous.
> But wonder at a greater wonder, for to us
> Created nature doth these things subdue,
> But their Creator, whom sin, nor nature tied,
> For us, His creatures, and His foes, hath died.[28]

28. John Donne, "Holy Sonnets," 12, in *Selected Poems* (Gramercy, 1994), 198.

Coda

Psalm 148

Translated by Ethan C. Jones

Praise the Lord.
    Praise the Lord from the heavens.
Praise him in the heights.
Praise him, all his angels.
    Praise him, all his heavenly hosts.
Praise him, you sun and moon.
    Praise him, all the stars of light.
Praise him, you highest of heavens
    and the waters above the heavens.
Let them praise the name of the Lord.
    For he decreed and they were created.
He made them stand sure forever.
    An order he gave—it will not wither.
Praise the Lord from the earth,
    sea creatures, and all the depths.
Lightning and hail, snow and mist,

the tempest wind does his word.
The mountains and every hill,
fruit tree and cedar alike,
creatures and every beast,
crawling thing and flying bird,
kings of the earth, and every nation,
princes, and every judge of the earth,
young men and maidens,
the aged along with youth,
let them all praise the name of the LORD.
For his name alone is high,
his splendor over earth and heavens.
He has raised the horn of his people.
Praise for all his devotees,
for the children of Israel,
a people near him.
Praise the LORD.

Acknowledgments

Here it is my pleasure to give honor where it is due. I am thankful to the series editors, Graham Cole and Oren Martin, for inviting me to write this volume and waiting patiently for the final product. The team at Crossway has been simply delightful. Jeff Griffin and Eric Benoy, of the John Christian Library at New Orleans Baptist Theological Seminary, swiftly and cheerfully acquired every book or article I asked for. Many others were helpful conversation partners along the way, including Steve Duby, Bobby Jamieson, Matthew Anderson, and Todd Hains. Thanks also to Ryan Modisette for tidying up the manuscript and double-checking my Latin translations.

Two folks deserve special mention, though. Kirsten Sanders challenged me to let go of some unwarranted prejudices about what theological writing should look like, which was as helpful as it was disruptive. And my friend and colleague Ethan Jones entertained my Old Testament and Hebrew questions tirelessly and generously translated Psalm 148 for this book's coda.

Thanks also to our church family at Immanuel Community Church in New Orleans, and to the many who prayed for my progress on this book and asked me questions along the way, not least of whom was Matthew DeLaughter. Finally, I am grateful for my wife, Jessie. In many ways, she shaped this book more than anyone else through our conversations prompted by her insightful questions. She is a constant reminder to me and our children of God's fruitful love.

Glossary

doxology. Any form of voiced praise.

economy. The orderly arrangement of God's eternal plan, which aims at and pursues a particular goal.

liturgy. When used in high church contexts, liturgy consists of the rituals and words that surround the Lord's Supper or Eucharist. And more broadly, it means the worship that adheres to a specific form regulated by Scripture. This broader meaning is often in view within Scripture when *liturgy* means the duties or office that renders a particular service to others, whether to God or to created persons. In the context of doxology in this book, liturgy is the orderly worship of God's people that answers to the order and purpose of creation itself. It includes prayer, ritual, offering of thanks, and praise to God, all prescribed by God's word (1 Chron. 16:4; Rom. 9:4; Heb. 9:1). Not only does it encompass the worship we offer to God, but it also embraces the whole of our lives (Rom. 12:1).

sacrifice. As used in this book, *sacrifice* carries the basic spiritualized meaning of acts of obedience that draw us near to God. This is similar to the meaning Augustine gives it, which is found in the argument of chapter 7. The term therefore embraces Old

Testament sacrifices as well as the "sacrifice" of thanksgiving and obedience found in the New Testament.

song. This book's central metaphor for creation and its economy in Scripture. *Original song* represents creation itself. In one respect, this metaphor designates creation as a reality "sung" into existence by God and shot through with harmony, rhythm, and form. In another respect, this same metaphor is used for how creatures harmonize with this original song through the instrumentality of their created lives. *New song* represents the redemption and eschatological fulfillment of creation in Christ.

Further Reading

Augustine. *City of God*. This sprawling masterpiece offers more than a doctrine of creation set in the context of doxology and spiritual warfare, but certainly not less. Within Augustine's vision of two opposed cities established by two contrary loves is a biblical theology of creation setting forth God's plan for how created goods relate to self, church, and society.

Blocher, Henri. *In the Beginning: The Opening Chapters of Genesis*. InterVarsity Press, 1984. A characteristically judicious discussion that is attentive to biblical exegesis and theology without losing one for the other.

Blowers, Paul M. *The Drama of the Divine Economy: Creator and Creation in Early Christian Theology and Piety*. Oxford University Press, 2012. A masterful exploration of the early church's interpretative approaches and doxological uses of the doctrine of creation. Blowers helpfully points readers to the primary texts with enough context to equip them to read the sources firsthand.

Brown, Andrew J. *Recruiting the Ancients for the Creation Debate*. Eerdmans, 2023. An impressive and mostly reliable introduction to how theologians interpreted the creation week from the early church through the Reformation, providing helpful context for current debates. As is almost always the case with broad studies, important details relevant to individual interpreters get lost.

Davison, Andrew. *Participation in God: A Study in Christian Doctrine and Metaphysics*. Cambridge University Press, 2019. The doctrine of "participation" is behind large swathes of Christian reflection on creation. The material may be demanding for many readers, but they will not find a clearer exposition of participation and its consequences for Christian thought than Davison provides.

Klink, Edward W., III. *The Beginning and End of All Things: A Biblical Theology of Creation and New Creation*. Essential Studies in Biblical Theology. IVP Academic, 2023. An accessible, pastoral exposition of creation that traces its associated themes and images through the various stages of God's plan. Klink's conclusions in favor of a "supralapsarian" Christology (i.e., the view that the Son would have become incarnate even apart from sin) do not necessarily follow from the evidence, but that takes nothing away from his lucid treatment.

Scheffczyk, Leo. *Creation and Providence*. The Herder History of Dogma. Herder and Herder, 1970. This book remains the best introduction to the history of the doctrine available in English.

General Index

Abel, 149, 156
Abraham, oath to, 128–29
Adam
as "from the ground," 105
liturgical commission of, 131, 149, 155
naming of animals, 148–50, 152
as son of God, 126
Adam and Eve, fell into disorder, 96, 116
Adams, Douglas, 51
adoption, 125n6
angelic praise, 58, 59
animals, study of, 150–52
art, 57n31
Athanasius, 50n17, 74n18, 83n7, 97, 98n34, 120n26
atheism, 72
Auer, Johann, 36n40
Augustine, 7, 12n2, 13, 25n22, 37, 43n4, 65n4, 75, 78n25, 82n6, 84n8, 87n14, 92n22, 93, 95n27, 116n21, 119n25, 157, 161–62n26, 162n27, 169, 171

Barth, Karl, 111n13, 152n11
Basil of Caesarea, 13, 67n6, 82n6, 87n14, 151n10
Bauckham, Richard, 117n22
Bavinck, Herman, 114, 118n23, 151
Beale, G. K., 52n21, 131nn14–15
Bekken, Perl Jarle, 126n8
Berry, Wendell, 106
biblical cosmology, 33–34
Blocher, Henri, 21n14, 36n40, 171
Blowers, Paul M., 151n9, 171
body and soul, 88–89, 90, 96
Bonaventure, 7, 84n8, 161n25
Bouttier, Michel, 124n4
Brown, Andrew J., 171
Burke, Trevor J., 125n8

Cain, 149, 156
Calvin, John, 51n20, 56n28, 151, 161n23
Canaan, 139
Carson, D. A., 81n3
church, consecrates creation, 162
clean and unclean, 158–59
Clement of Alexandria, 3–4
common and holy, 158
communal bonds, 104–5, 117
consummation of creation, 4, 52
Cotter, David W., 153n15

creation
abuse of, 154–55
as act of God's freedom, 47–50
of "all things," 65
care for, 113–14
clarity about, 40
consecration of, 155–62
disorder of, 74, 117, 134, 135
distinctions in, 152
divinization of, 155
as doxological, 6, 8, 23, 29, 32, 37, 132
flourishing of, 52–53
glorifies God, 55, 107–9, 115
goodness of, 22
harmony of, 7–8, 53, 93–99
as inheritance, 125–30
inseparable from redemption and glorification, 57
intrinsic and extrinsic ends of, 53–56
liturgical form of, 24–25
not arbitrary, 51
not a battleground of the gods, 73
not necessary, 50
order of, 33, 35, 112–13
personification of, 31
purposes and end of, 52–59
as song, 1–3, 7, 59, 102, 130–31
spoken by God, 83–84, 85
structured space of, 22–23
vanity of, 115–20
creation out of nothing, 7, 62, 63–66, 70, 78
Creator-creation distinction, 23–24, 68–71
Creator-creation relation, 71–74
creatures
agency of, 76–77
different ends of, 112–15
distinctions among, 90–91, 110
intrinsic goodness and worth of, 76
wholeness of, 85–86, 93, 97
crown of honor, 141
Cyril of Alexandria, 96n31, 46, 125n7

Davidson, Ivor J., 137n22
Davison, Andrew, 63nn1–2, 74n19, 172
Day of Atonement, 132
deism, 8
demons, 69–70
desire
of creatures, 54–55
in God, 43
Desmond, William, 27n23
dietary laws, 158–59
dominion, 146–55
Donne, John, 163n28
doxology of creation, 58, 103–9, 130–31, 169

economy, 122, 169
Eden, expansion of, 116
Enuma Elish, 73
eternal life, 128, 135, 139–40
Eve, as helper, 153n15
evil, as an absence, 63n1

false gods, 70
false teachers, 160
Ferguson, Everett, 156n18
festivals of Israel, 18–19
Filtvedt, Ole Jakob, 133n19

forming and filling pattern of creation week, 20–22, 96n29
framework view of creation week, 20n13
fruitfulness of creation, 66, 105–7, 109, 110
fruit of the Spirit, 107

genealogies, 108
generations, 103–4
"generations" sayings, 32–33n35
geocentric view, 9
glorification, 52, 57, 103
God
- artistry of, 66–67
- clarity about, 40
- communication with creatures, 75–76
- created "all things," 62–63
- created everything for his own glory, 57–58
- creative freedom of, 47–51
- decree of, 56
- delight in his own goodness, 55
- direct and indirect forms of creating, 66
- dominion of, 146–47
- economy of, 122
- as Father of lights, 127
- forming what he speaks, 94–96
- freedom to create, 49–51
- fruitfulness of, 41, 46, 59, 107–8
- fullness of, 41, 48, 75–76
- generosity in creation, 62, 74–78, 148, 162
- glory of, 17, 56, 84, 115, 137, 154, 161
- goodness of, 41–44, 47
- internal and external works of, 48–49
- lordship of, 50
- musicality of, 39, 41, 44–49, 51, 52, 59, 61, 78, 83–84, 107, 138, 140
- necessary and contingent works of, 48–49
- patience of, 78
- peace of, 30
- power of, 78
- presence in new Jerusalem, 137
- propensity to share himself, 44–45
- relation to creation, 68
- rest of, 30, 138, 140–41
- song of, 61–67
- sovereignty of, 67, 74, 77
- speaks creation into significance, 78, 81–83
- as transcendent and immanent, 70–71
- wisdom of, 51, 56, 78

Goldingay, John, 116n20
goodness
- of creatures, 76
- as desirable and communicative, 42–44

grace, 52, 139
gratitude, 148, 153–55
- as liturgy of Christian living, 161
- and sacrifice, 158

Gregory of Nyssa, 84n8
Grosseteste, Robert, 141n28
growth, 126

Hahn, Scott W., 125n8
Hamann, J. G., v
harmony, of Word and Spirit, 96–99
heavenly Jerusalem, 140
heliocentric model, 9

hexaemeron, 11
  doxological rhythm of, 15–20, 37
  as a hymn, 12–15, 25–27, 37
  poetry of, 14, 37
  as prophetic speech, 13–14
  spatial pattern of, 20–24
  temple imagery of, 27–30
Hildegard of Bingen, 119n25
human disorder, 115–20
human dominion, 146–47, 154–55
humans, humanity
  as conductors of creation, 8, 110
  and corruption of creation, 116
  dignity of, 57–58
  distinct from other creatures, 111
  of one kind, 111–12
  as parable son, 129

idols, idolatry, 70, 73, 87, 118, 155
image bearers, 8, 112, 120
immediate creation, 66n5
inanimate creatures, 55, 76, 109
inheritance, 128, 130–35, 137–38
Israel
  as firstborn son, 126
  liturgy of, 131–33
  sacrifices of, 156–57
  worship of, 19

Jacob of Serug, 14n6
Jenson, Robert W., 147n1
Jesus Christ
  at center of creation, 4, 99, 122
  as creation's melody, 7, 125, 129
  with crown of thorns, 141
  frees creation from futility, 122
  as heir of creation, 135
  leads us in inheriting land and rest, 128
  liturgical fulfillment of creation, 133–35, 145, 160
  mediatorial work of, 99
  as new song, 3
  orchestra's new conductor, 133–34
  reconciles world to himself, 123–25
  restores song and sonship, 129
  sacrifice of, 134, 157–58
  temptations of, 127–28
  see also Word of God
Job, 152
John of Damascus, 46n12, 71n11
Jubilee, 132, 135
Judas, 159n21
Junius, Franciscus, 55n27, 57n29, 58n33

Kaufmann, Yehezkel, 72n15
Ken, Thomas, 101
Kleinig, John W., 134n20, 136n21
Klink, Edward W., III, 82n5, 172
knowledge of the Trinity, 59

ladder imagery, 56–57
LeFebvre, Michael, 18n10, 20n11
Leigh, Edward, 151n10
Leithart, Peter J., 148n2, 160n22, 161n24
Lessius, Leonardus, 46n11
Lewis, C. S., 3n3, 114n17
light, as metaphor for God's glory, 16–17
liturgical calendar, 20
liturgical chant, 5
liturgy, 24–25, 169
living sacrifice, 158
logos, 81

Lord's Supper, 134, 159
Luther, Martin, 13, 14, 84n9, 85nn10–12, 149

Marduk, 73
marriage, 66
Mastricht, Petrus van, 44nn5–6, 46n10, 48n16
material causality, 67n7, 77n22
materialism, 8
Maximus the Confessor, 84n8
McDonough, Sean M., 33n37
mediate creation, 66n5
Melchizedek, 128–29
melody, 79
Miller, Patrick D., 32n33
Morales, L. Michael, 115n18, 131n14
Mount Zion, 140

naming in Scripture, 148–49
naturalism, 72
new covenant, purity in, 159
new creation, 56, 146
  glory of, 136–38
  rest of, 138–42
new heavens and new earth, 29, 140
new Jerusalem, 137, 146
new song, 3–6, 27, 52, 56, 128, 130, 142–43, 145–46, 162, 170
nonhuman creatures, 105, 119, 151, 152

obedience, 156
O'Donovan, Oliver, 32n34, 110n12, 153n16
"orchestra" of creatures, 7, 109–10, 112
order of love, 88n16
Origen, 87n14
original song, 56, 162, 170

pagan religions, creation accounts of, 72–74
pantheism, 8
peace, 25, 30
Pennington, Jonathan T., 33n37
Pieper, Josef, 139n24
poetry, 30–32
  reveals and conceals, 34–36
  teaches order and meaning, 32–34
polytheism, 73
prodigal son, 129
promised land, 128
prophets, 14
prose poetry, 14
providence, 56, 77n23
purity, 159

Radner, Ephraim, 104, 132n16, 151n9
Ratzinger, Joseph, 73, 90n19, 111n13
recapitulation, 20n12, 123, 125
redemption, 4–5, 52, 57
remembering the Creator, 36, 73
rest, 128, 132, 138–42

Sabbath, 18–19, 28, 132, 139
sabbatical year, 132
sacrifice, 134, 155–63, 169–70
satanic powers, deform creation, 69
Scheeben, Matthias Joseph, 46n15
Scheffczyk, Leo, 172
Schmitz, Kenneth L., 148n2
science, 35–36

Scripture
  and science, 8, 36
  symbolic cosmological language of, 33–34
seventh day, 17, 18, 19, 30, 115, 135, 138–39
Sokolowski, Robert, 71nn12–13
Solomon, 152
Son, harmony of, 95
song, 170. *See also* creation, as song; new song; original song
song of the Lamb. *See* new song
son of God, 126
son of man, 125
sonship, 125–26, 129
space, in creation, 22–23
spoken creatures, echo the spoken God, 84
suffering, 142
suppressing knowledge, 87
Swete, Henry Barclay, 52n21

tabernacle, 17, 28–29
teachability, 13–14
temple imagery, 27–30
thankfulness. *See* gratitude
Theophylact of Ohrid, 95n26
Thomas Aquinas, 40n2, 45n8, 50n18, 53n23, 54n24, 55nn25–26, 57n30, 58n32, 59n36, 90n19, 124n4, 141n29
Tolkien, J. R. R., 1–2, 3, 5
Trinity
  acts indivisibly in creation, 69
  communication within himself, 75
  fruitful life of love, 44–47
  see also God
true self, 90, 91
Turretin, Francis, 66n5, 96n30

Voetius, Gisbertus, 76n22
Vogels, Walter, 18n9
Volk, Hermann, 98n36

Wenham, Gordon, 24n20
wholeness
  horizontal axis of, 87–90
  vertical axis of, 86, 87, 88–90
Wirzba, Norman, 105n7, 106, 151n9, 153n14
wisdom, 150, 152–54
Word of God
  and creation, 7, 62–63, 78, 80–84
  forgiveness and mercy through, 135
  as God's complete self-revelation, 81
worship, 17–18, 93

Yom Kippur, 132, 133

Zuckerkandl, Victor, 94n25

Scripture Index

Genesis
book of 7, 12, 33n35
1 .... 82n5
1–2 .... 32n33
1:1 .... 62, 81
1:1–2:4 11
1:2 .... 20, 28n24, 65, 94
1:3 .... 28n25, 81n4
1:3–5 .... 21, 22
1:3–31 94
1:4 .... 29n29
1:5 16
1:6 .... 28n25, 29n29
1:6–7 .... 81n4
1:6–8 .... 21, 22, 28
1:7 .... 29, 29n29
1:8 16
1:9 .... 28n25, 81n4
1:9–13 .... 21, 22
1:10 22
1:11 .... 81n4, 111
1:11–12 .... 24, 110
1:12 .... 22, 110
1:13 16
1:14 .... 18, 28n25, 29n29
1:14–15 .... 29, 81n4
1:14–19 .... 21, 22
1:16 17
1:18 .... 29n29
1:19 16
1:20 .... 28n25, 29, 81n4, 111
1:20–23 .... 21, 22
1:21 .... 24, 28n27, 110
1:22 .... 108n10, 110
1:23 16
1:24 .... 28n25, 81n4, 111
1:24–25 .... 24, 110
1:24–31 .... 21, 22
1:25 22
1:26 .... 28n25, 115
1:26–28 128
1:26–30 .... 81n4
1:27 .... 24, 29, 87, 111, 112
1:28 .... 108n10, 126, 153n15
1:29 .... 66, 114
1:31 .... 16, 22, 74, 76, 161
2:1 21

2:1–3 . . . . 21, 28n27, 29
2:2 . . . . 18, 30, 132
2:2–3 . . . . 28n27, 126, 138, 139, 140n27
2:3 . . . . 22, 138
2:4 . . . . 32n35, 104
2:7 . . . . 65, 105, 111
2:15 . . . . 66, 126, 131, 131n15, 149
2:16 105
2:16–17 152
2:16–19 66
2:18 . . . . 148, 153n15
2:19 111
2:20 153
2:23 . . . . 148, 150n6
2:24 66
3–11 . . . . 24, 89
3:1 . . . . 91, 116n21, 131
3:2–3 120
3:4–5 . . . . 127n10
3:8 119
3:15 117
3:16 . . . . 117, 124
3:17 117
3:17–18 105
3:17–19 66
3:18 141
3:19 105
3:20 148
4:1 . . . . 149n3
4:1–2 148
4:3–4 156
5:1 . . . . 33n35, 103
6:1–4 89
6:9 . . . . 33n35, 103, 104
6:12 116
6:13–17 66
7:1 104
7:11 29
8:17 . . . . 108n10, 110
8:22 20
9:1 . . . . 108n10
9:2–3 114
9:3 147
9:7 . . . . 108n10
10:1 . . . . 33n35, 103
11:10 . . . . 33n35
11:27 . . . . 33n35
12:1 88
12:7 128
14:17–24 . . . . 128n13
14:22 147
15:7–8 . . . . 128n11
15:18 . . . . 128n12
15:18–21 . . . . 128n11
17:15–21 . . . . 128n11
22:16–18 . . . . 128n12
22:18 128
28:3 . . . . 108n10

Exodus

3:8 . . . . 126n9
4:22–23 126
8:1 18
18:4 . . . . 153n15
19:5 147
19:6 . . . . 126, 158
20:5 104
20:6 131
20:8–11 . . . . 18, 138
20:11 . . . . 30, 140n27
20:17 54
24:16 28
25:1 . . . . 28n25

25:20 29
25:30–31 17
25:31–40 29
26:7 28
26:33 . . . . .28, 29n29
28:1 29
28:36–38 3
30:11 . . . . .28n25
30:17 . . . . .28n25
30:17–21 29
30:22 . . . . .28n25
30:34 . . . . .28n25
31:1 . . . . .28n25
31:3 . . . . .28n24
31:12 . . . . .28n25
31:12–17 . . . . .28n27
31:17 . . . . .140n27, 141
32:1–6 . . . . .127n10
33:19 45
34:6–7 45
34:13–16 . . . . .111n14
35:8 17
35:14 17
35:28 17
35:31 . . . . .28n24
39:32 . . . . .28n27, 29
39:43 . . . . .28n27, 29
40:4 17
40:9–11 . . . . .28n27
40:33–34 . . . . .28n27

Leviticus
1–7 28
1:1 132
1:17 . . . . .29n29
5:8 . . . . .29n29
8:33 28
9:23 . . . . .132, 157
10:1–2 116
10:10 . . . . .29n29
10:10–11 158
11 158
11:42 131
11:47 . . . . .29n29
16:15 132
16:29 132
16:30 133
16:31 . . . . .132, 132n17
18:24 159
19:19 . . . . .24, 111n14
20:22–27 159
20:24–26 . . . . .29n29
23 . . . . .18n9, 19, 20n12, 155
23:5 . . . . .18n10
23:6–8 . . . . .18n10
23:9–14 . . . . .18n10
23:15–22 . . . . .18n10
23:22 18
23:23–25 . . . . .18n10
23:26–32 . . . . .18n10
23:33–44 . . . . .18n10
25:1–7 116
25:4 132
25:4–7 132
25:8–55 . . . . .19, 132
25:55 132
26:6 117
27:29 146

Numbers
3:7–8 131
6:24–26 17
6:27 146
8:1–4 17
8:14 . . . . .29n29
8:26 131
16:9 . . . . .29n29

18:5–6 131
18:20 140
34:2 .... 126n9

Deuteronomy
4:21 126
5:1 .... 131, 149
5:14 116
5:16–21 104
5:32–33 127
6:4–5 93
6:5 .... 123n2
7:3–4 .... 111n14
7:26 146
12:9 .... 30n31, 126
12:10 139
22:9–11 24
28:4 107
30:14 93
32:6 149
32:17 70
33:7 .... 153n15
33:26–29 .... 153n15

Joshua
1:8 127
11:22 .... 126n9
21:43–45 128
22:2–4 .... 126n9
23:12–13 .... 111n14
24:14–15 .... 127n10

1 Samuel
15:22 156
16:23 3

2 Samuel
7:1 .... 30n31, 128
7:2–27 .... 128n11
7:8–16 .... 128n13
12:7 123
16:14 141

1 Kings
4:33 152
5:3–4 .... 30n31
5:4 128
7:49 17
8:56 .... 30n31, 132
9:6 131
11:1–2 .... 111n14

2 Kings
14:21 .... 153n15

1 Chronicles
6:31 132
6:31–48 3
16:4 169
17:3–15 .... 128n11

2 Chronicles
26:1 .... 153n15

Ezra
9:1–2 .... 111n14

Job
7:16 149
9:8 29
12:7–8 152
26:11 29
26:12 31
26:13 .... 69, 94
33:4 94
35:11 119
36:24 v
36:27–28 66

38–41 152
38:4–11 35
38:7 .... 5, 26
38:8–9 31
38:37 31

Psalms
book of 14
1:3 .... 66, 107, 150
1:6 27
2:8 128
8:4–6 .... 120, 125
8:5 141
10:11 72
13 142
16:2 .... 58, 75, 140
16:11 140
19 55
19:1 .... 31n32
19:1–3 87
19:4 87
21:6 140
22:22 134
24:1 147
25:8 42
27:4 58
27:6 162
28:7 141
29:9 58
32:9 119
33:3 .... 4n8
33:6 .... 69, 82, 94
33:8–9 26
33:9 .... 67, 78
33:11 136
34:8 .... 42, 55, 58
34:10 42
36:9 138
40:3 .... 4n8
42:2 42
46:1 .... 153n15
50:6 .... 31n32
50:7–15 50
50:10–11 75
50:10–12 147
50:12–15 156
50:23 161
51:10 69
51:16–17 156
65:8 .... 101n1
65:12–13 .... 31n32, 101n1
68:16 .... 43n4
69:30 161
69:34 .... 101n1
73:25 42
74:13–17 31
78:23 29
78:69 29
89:3–4 .... 128n11, 128n13
89:9–10 31
89:12 .... 101n1
89:27–29 .... 128n11
89:36 136
94:9 .... 96n29
95:5 .... 65, 96n29
95:7–11 141
95:11 127
96:1 .... 4n8, 68
96:5 70
96:8 160
96:12–13 .... 101n1
98:1 .... 4n8
103:5 58
103:21 108
104 .... 8, 12
104:1 27
104:2 .... 16, 28, 29, 31

104:5 31
104:9 23
104:10–13 66
104:10–15 23
104:11–12 113
104:14–15 113
104:16–18 113
104:24 .... 26, 51, 153
104:30 69
104:33 27
104:35 27
106:37 70
107:20 .... 81n3
110:4 128
111:3 136
111:10 136
113:9 103
115:3 67
115:16 .... 114, 147
116:7 141
117:2 136
119:9–10 89
119:68 44
119:89 .... 84, 91
126:5–6 92
127:3 103
128 107
132:8 .... 30, 132
132:13–14 .... 43n4, 140
135:6 67
139:13 149
139:13–15 87
139:16 .... 87, 91, 96n29
144:4 149
144:9 .... 4n8
145:7 58
145:9 42
145:15–16 55
145:16 42
146:2 102
147:11 162
147:15 .... 66, 78
148 .... 8, 27, 31n32, 55, 102, 165
148:1 102
148:5 82
148:6 23
149:4 162
150:6 102

Proverbs
2:10 153
3:19 .... 23, 51, 153
3:19–20 .... 28n24
6:6–8 150
8:22–31 23
8:24 65
26:3 119
30:28 150
31:17 .... 153n15
31:25 .... 153n15

Ecclesiastes
1:2 .... 115, 149
1:4 34
1:7 66
1:8 35
1:9 34
3:11 92
3:20 111
12:1 73
12:13–14 92

Song of Solomon
1:3 145

Isaiah
1:3 . . . 151
2:2–4 . . . 116
6:1–5 . . . 146
6:3 . . . 107, 138
9:6 . . . 59
9:8 . . . 81n3
24:4 . . . 117n22
27:6 . . . 107
29:15 . . . 72
32:9–20 . . . 107
33:9 . . . 117n22
35:1–2 . . . 58
35:2 . . . 108
40:1–5 . . . 58
40:8 . . . 136
40:9–31 . . . 67
40:12 . . . 31
40:12–17 . . . 71
40:15 . . . 31
40:19 . . . 70
40:22 . . . 29
40:25 . . . 71
40:28 . . . 140
42:8 . . . 138
42:10 . . . 4n8
43:1 . . . 96n29
43:6–7 . . . 54n24
43:7 . . . 96n29
44:2 . . . 96n29
44:24 . . . 68, 96n29
45:7 . . . 65
45:12 . . . 68
45:18 . . . 21
46:5 . . . 71
46:9–10 . . . 49
48:11 . . . 54n24
55:11 . . . 78, 81n3
55:12 . . . 101n1
58:13 . . . 19
60:1 . . . 16
60:1–22 . . . 137
60:19 . . . 17
60:20 . . . 137
61:1–3 . . . 135
65:16 . . . 85
66:1–2 . . . 29
66:1–23 . . . 140

Jeremiah
1:4 . . . 81n3
4:23–28 . . . 117n22
5:22 . . . 31
6:16 . . . 141
9:12–14 . . . 117n22
10:10–16 . . . 67
12:4 . . . 117n22
17:9 . . . 54
18:1–11 . . . 65
23:10 . . . 117n22

Lamentations
2:14 . . . 120

Ezekiel
13:1–8 . . . 120
19:10–14 . . . 107
33:7 . . . 81n3
34:25–31 . . . 118
43:7 . . . 137
48:35 . . . 137

Daniel
7:14 . . . 125

Hosea
4:1–3 . . . 117
6:6 . . . 156
14:4–8 . . . 107

Joel
1:10 ....117n22

Amos
1:2..................117n22
1:3–2:3.............111n14
4:13 31
9:6..................31

Micah
6:6–8...............156

Haggai
2:4–5...............137
2:6..................136
2:7..................137

Zechariah
2:5..................137
8:12–13............118

Matthew
1:1..................104
1:3–5...............111n14
3:8..................126
4:1..................141
4:4..................127, 127n10
4:8..................127
5:16 107
6:10 136
6:26 114
6:34 92
10:16...............151
10:29–31 114
11:2–6 135
11:28...............141
11:29...............93
12:11–12 114
12:33...............46
12:34...............84
13:17...............142
15:18...............83
16:25...............162
19:12...............88
19:17...............42
22:30...............108
22:36–40 78
22:37–40 ....123n2
26:39...............88
27:24–61 105
28:18...............128, 129

Mark
2:27 ....19, 138
4:15 89
4:35–41............80
4:39 ....82n5, 98
5:1–20 89
5:21–43............105
7:1–23 159
7:19 161
10:9 90
10:18...............58
10:21–22 161
12:28–31 123

Luke
2:14 59
2:52 126
3:38 126
11:11–13 127
11:41–42 156
14:26...............88
15:7 129
15:12–16 129
15:17...............129
15:18...............129
15:18–20 ....95n28

15:21 . . . 129
15:31 . . . 129
15:32 . . . 129
19:10 . . . 57

John
book of . . . 62, 80n1
1:1 . . . 81, 95, 95n28
1:1–3 . . . 63
1:1–4 . . . 80
1:3 . . . 3, 63, 69, 74, 80n1, 82n5, 125n6
1:4 . . . 84, 95
1:9 . . . 17
1:9–14 . . . 16
1:12–13 . . . 125n6
1:14 . . . 63, 80, 81, 82, 99
1:17 . . . 63
1:18 . . . 80, 81, 84, 95
2:22 . . . 82
3:16–17 . . . 95
3:16–18 . . . 81
4:39 . . . 83
5:17 . . . 30, 83, 99
5:19 . . . 95
5:22–24 . . . 81
5:26 . . . 94, 99
6:32–58 . . . 95
8:44 . . . 116n21
8:47 . . . 127
10:10 . . . 95
11:17–37 . . . 105
11:25 . . . 95
11:43 . . . 83, 97
12:16 . . . 82
12:24 . . . 95, 122
12:25 . . . 161
12:28 . . . 138
13:1 . . . 157
13:2 . . . 159n21
13:27 . . . 159n21
14:1–3 . . . 95
14:6 . . . 93, 95
14:9 . . . 84
14:23 . . . 95
14:26 . . . 82
15:3 . . . 135, 159n21
15:4 . . . 126
15:4–5 . . . 108
15:4–7 . . . 95
15:5 . . . 95
15:8 . . . 107
15:11 . . . 95
16:15 . . . 84, 129
16:28 . . . 95
17:1–5 . . . 128
17:5 . . . 138
17:14–19 . . . 112n14
17:17–19 . . . 158
17:22 . . . 55
17:24 . . . 83, 95, 138
19:5 . . . 124
20:29–31 . . . 142

Acts
4:24 . . . 69
4:28 . . . 49
10:9–16 . . . 159
14:15 . . . 118
15:20 . . . 159
15:28 . . . 159
16:1 . . . 112n14
17:22 . . . 73
17:24–25 . . . 50
17:25 . . . 75
17:26 . . . 88, 111

17:26–28 104
17:28 .... 71, 80n1

Romans
1:3 129
1:18 152
1:20 87
1:21 .... 118, 120, 148
1:23 87
1:24–25 89
1:25 .... 24, 70, 72
1:26 90
1:26–27 87
3:4 92
4:13 128
4:17 74
8:2 97
8:15–21 .... 125n6
8:17 .... 125, 130, 137
8:18 .... 92, 120, 138
8:19 119
8:19–21 118
8:19–22 .... 31n32, 57
8:20 115
8:20–22 74
8:21–23 138
8:22 63
8:24 120
8:29 .... 96n29, 119
8:30 .... 55, 138
9:4 169
9:20–21 65
10:8 93
11:16 .... 112n14
11:36 .... 56, 58, 62, 63, 80n1
12:1 .... 158, 169
12:1–2 97
12:2 93
12:5 124
13:8 154
13:9 .... 123n2
14:7–8 162
14:13–23 160
14:14 159
16:27 .... 58n34

1 Corinthians
1:9 .... 80n1
1:18 133
3:7 107
3:16–17 90
4:7 .... 75, 154
5:9–11 .... 111n14
6:15–20 90
7:1–5 89
7:12–16 .... 112n14
8:4 70
8:5 70
8:6 .... 63, 69, 80, 80n1
9:17 .... 122n1
10:1–22 89
10:16–18 .... 159n21
10:20 70
10:23–11:1 160
11:11–12 91
11:12 .... 91n20
11:14 91
11:27 .... 159n21
11:27–32 159
11:29 .... 159n21
13:4 36
14:33 25
14:40 25
15:28 145
15:39–41 111
15:41 108
15:43 135

2 Corinthians
1:17–20 89
1:20 4
3:17 97
4:6.................. 16, 17, 135
5:17 5
5:19 124
6:14–18 .... 111n14
9:13 157
12:7 88
12:10............... 141

Galatians
3:16 129
3:28 124
3:28–29 124
4:4.................. 123
4:19 .... 96n29
5:1.................. 97
5:22–24 107
6:15 5

Ephesians
1:5–6 56
1:9.................. 122
1:10 .... 20n12, 122n1, 123, 124
1:11 .... 49, 50, 51
1:11–12 56
1:14 56
1:22–23 124
1:23 76
2:11–19 124
2:14 .... 88n15
3:9.................. 63, 69, 122n1
3:21 .... 58n34
4:4.................. 124
4:13 126
4:17 120
4:17–18 118
5:19 125
5:32 91

Philippians
2:7.................. 96n29, 97, 157
2:13 77
3:19 152
3:21 .... 96n29, 119
4:13 141
4:18 157
4:20 .... 58n34

Colossians
1:15–17 69
1:15–20 26
1:16 .... 20n12, 80, 80n1, 121, 125
1:16–17 63
1:17 .... 74, 125
1:18 99
1:20 124
2:3.................. 84
2:17 .... 20n12, 133, 156
3:16 143

1 Timothy
1:4.................. 122
1:15 57
1:17 .... 58n34
2:5.................. 99n37
4:1–3 160
4:3.................. 161
4:4–5 160
6:15 .... 45, 140
6:16 16

Titus
1:15 160

Hebrews
1:2 .... 69, 125, 130
1:3 .... 84, 95, 133, 141
1:5–14 .... 128n13
1:5–2:18 .... 128n11
1:7 108
1:10 69
2:5 134
2:8 142
2:8–9 130
2:9 125
2:10 .... 80, 80n1, 141
2:11 .... 129, 134
2:12 134
2:16 129
2:17 130
3:1–14 141
3:6 130
4:1–10 141
4:1–11 .... 132n17
4:3 139
4:7 .... 135, 145
4:9 139
4:9–10 19
4:10 139
4:11 141
4:12–13 139
4:14 142
4:15 129
4:16 .... 130, 142
5:5–10 .... 128n13
5:9 134
6:14–15 .... 128n12
6:15 127
6:19–20 141
6:20 .... 128n13
7:3 129
7:11 133
7:16 129
7:19 134
7:22 134
7:27–28 133
8:2 130
8:6 .... 129, 133
9:1 169
9:12 .... 129, 134
9:14 134
9:15 .... 99n37, 134
10:4 133
10:5 156
10:10 .... 134, 158
10:34 134
10:35 130
11:3 142
11:8 .... 128n12
11:8–16 133
11:16 134
11:32–38 88
11:39–40 142
12:22 140
12:22–24 142
12:24 .... 134, 145
12:25–29 99
12:26 136
12:27 136
13:8 145
13:15–16 157
13:20 134
13:21 .... 58, 58n34

James
1:5 153
1:17 .... 42, 127, 153
1:17–18 50
2:10 .... 118n23
4:13–15 92
4:14 115

1 Peter
1:18 120
1:18–19 134
2:5. . . . . .134, 158
2:9. . . . . .97, 158
3:7. . . . . .153n15
4:11 . . . . .58n34

2 Peter
2:4. . . . . .116n21
3:5. 65
3:18 . . . . .58n34

1 John
1:1–2. 82
1:5. 17
2:8. 17
2:16 119
3:2. 98
3:8. 57
4:1–6. 119
4:7–12 94
4:8. 46

Jude
25. . . . . .58n34

Revelation
book of 4, 5, 69
1:6. . . . . .58n34
3:12 146
3:14 85
4:11 . . . . .5, 6, 26, 40, 47, 52, 58, 58n34
5 . . . . .20n12
5:9–10 4
5:11–13. . . . . .27, 58n34
5:13 163
7:15 146
11:4 17
11:18. 69
12:9 . . . . .116n21
14:3 . . . . .4, 27, 143
19:2 69
21–22 29
21:1 136
21:3 137
21:5 . . . . .5, 120
21:7–8 160
21:22–23 137
21:22–27 160
21:23. . . . . .17, 98, 135, 146
21:27. 146
22:3 146
22:3–4 137
22:4 146
22:5 . . . . .17, 94
22:13. 121
22:20. 120

Short Studies in Systematic Theology

The Atonement
JEREMY TREAT

The Attributes of God
GERALD BRAY

The Church
GREGG R. ALLISON

Creation
TYLER R. WITTMAN

The Doctrine of Scripture
MARK D. THOMPSON

Glorification
GRAHAM A. COLE

The Holy Spirit
FRED SANDERS

Justification
THOMAS R. SCHREINER

The Person of Christ
STEPHEN J. WELLUM

Predestination
ANDREW DAVID NASELLI

Theological Method
GRAHAM A. COLE

The Trinity
SCOTT R. SWAIN

GRAHAM A. COLE AND OREN R. MARTIN, SERIES EDITORS